Getting into
Engineering Courses

Getting Into guides

Titles in this series

Getting into Art & Design Courses, 7th edition
Getting into Business & Economics Courses, 9th edition
Getting into Dental School, 7th edition
Getting into Law, 8th edition
Getting into Medical School 2012 Entry, 16th edition
Getting into Oxford & Cambridge 2012 Entry, 14th edition
Getting into Physiotherapy Courses, 5th edition
Getting into Psychology Courses, 8th edition
Getting into US & Canadian Universities, 2nd edition
Getting into Veterinary School, 8th edition
How to Complete Your UCAS Application 2012 Entry, 23rd edition

Getting into

Engineering Courses

James Burnett

trotman | **t**

Getting into Engineering Courses

This first edition published in 2011 by Trotman Publishing, an imprint of Crimson Publishing, Westminster House, Kew Road, Richmond, Surrey TW9 2ND.

© Trotman Publishing 2011

Author: James Burnett

British Library Cataloguing in Publication Data
A catalogue record of this book is available from the British Library.

ISBN: 978 1 84455 424 9

Typeset by IDSUK (Data Connection) Ltd.
Printed and bound in the UK by Ashford Colour Press, Gosport, Hants.

Contents

About the author		vii
Acknowledgements		ix
Introduction		**1**
	About this book	1
	Engineering defined	2
1|	**Choosing your course**	**9**
	What to consider	9
	Engineering courses	11
	The importance of mathematics	13
	League tables	13
	Entrance examinations	15
	Choosing the right course	16
	Placements and overseas study	18
	Methods of assessment and study	18
	Combined honours courses	18
	Other courses	20
	Academic and career-related factors	21
	Non-academic considerations	22
	Sources of finance	23
	Suggested timescale	28
2|	**Completing your UCAS application**	**31**
	Competition for places	31
	The UCAS application	32
	The personal statement	34
	Work experience	49
3|	**Work experience and the gap year**	**51**
	Work experience	51
	Looking for work experience	52
	A sample CV	53
	The covering letter	54
	Work experience interviews	55
	Taking a gap year	56

Contents

4| Succeeding at interview   **59**

Steering the interview   60
Preparation for an interview   61
The interview   63
How to answer interview questions   66

5| Non-standard applications   **71**

Mature students   71
International students   72

6| What happens next   **75**

Replies from the universities   75
Results day   75
What to do if things go wrong during the exams   76
Clearing   77
Adjustment   78
Retaking your A levels   79

7| Further training, qualifications and careers   **81**

Chartered engineer status   85
Master's courses   85

8| Current issues   **89**

Engineering disasters   89
The world's tallest building   90
Rare earth elements   91
Alternative sources of energy   91
Engineering business case histories   93

9| Further information   **95**

The UCAS tariff   95
Useful contacts   98
Books   100

About the author

James Burnett is a Director of Studies and careers and university adviser at Mander Portman Woodward. He has written and edited a number of the Trotman/MPW guides including *Getting into Art & Design Courses* and *Getting into Business & Economics Courses*; he is also a regular contributor to the education pages of the national newspapers and specialist careers publications.

Acknowledgements

I would like to thank Dolly Duan, who co-wrote some sections of this book, and undertook the research for many more: without her work there would be no book. The help given to me by Dominic Joyeux and Isabelle Kihm from, respectively, the Royal Academy of Engineering and the Institution of Mechanical Engineers; Emma Weeks from Bristol University; and Professor Stepan Lucyszyn from Imperial College was invaluable. Thank you also to Ben Goodrich, Alexandra Jackson, Josh Flower and Gulnaz Niyazova, who will undoubtedly follow highly successful careers in engineering, for allowing me to use their UCAS personal statements; and to Nigel Brook. I am grateful for the assistance of UCAS and to the universities which contributed advice or information.

James Burnett

Introduction

Engineering touches all aspects of our lives. Some of the work of engineers is easy to see and to understand – the electricity supply to your home, the car that drives you to school, the iPod you listen to on the way, the roads and bridges that take you to your destination, the school building and the classroom furniture you use, the water supply, the packaging for the food you eat at lunchtime, the computer you use to help you with your homework . . . the list is endless. But there are other aspects of engineering that you may not have thought about. Engineers also deal with financial and business issues, for example looking at the cost-effectiveness of manufacturing products; and many engineers run their own businesses. Engineers are closely involved in environmental and safety issues, as well as helping to shape the world's future energy and raw material needs.

Engineers are not often portrayed as glamorous figures. The public perception is of the person in oil-stained overalls wearing a hard hat and a luminous jacket, very often called in when there are problems (oil spills, power cuts, and damaged buildings and bridges spring to mind). There are not many films that have engineers as their leading characters (except for a string of blockbuster disaster movies from the 1970s), and when most people think about, for example, a stunning new building, it is the architect's name that comes to mind rather than the structural engineers who made it possible; when Apple introduces a new iPhone, we read articles about Steve Jobs rather than about the electronic and materials engineers who created it; and as you browse the web and come across an exciting website, you praise the web designer rather than the software engineers who developed the program that allowed the designer to weave their magic.

About this book

The aim of this book is to take you through the process of applying to study engineering, from choosing courses and universities through to postgraduate courses and career opportunities.

Chapter 1 focuses on choosing the right course and on the financial aspects of studying at university. Then in Chapter 2 we look at how to complete the all-important UCAS application, in particular, the personal statement section. In Chapter 3 we look at how you can gain work experience, which would be a valuable asset to your application, and ideas for gap years. Chapter 4 looks at the interview process for university and how to make a great impression on admissions tutors.

Chapter 5 provides information for mature applicants and international students.

Issues relating to examination results (including what to do if you do not get the grades you require) are discussed in Chapter 6; Chapter 7 covers postgraduate courses and professional qualifications; and Chapters 8 and 9 deal with current engineering issues and sources of further information.

However, my advice is to read the book from the beginning rather than dipping in and out of it, because you will then get a more complete picture. Throughout the book the examples that quote university entrance requirements use A level and AS level grades. But the advice is also applicable to students taking other qualifications such as Scottish Highers, the International Baccalaureate, and the Cambridge Pre-University. The UCAS website (www.ucas.com), in its Course Search section, lists entrance requirements for all of the major examination systems. If you are unsure about what you need to achieve, contact the universities you are interested in applying to for advice. Contact details are given on all the university websites.

Engineering defined

What is engineering?

What is the difference between science and engineering? There are many definitions, but essentially, engineering is the practical application of mathematics and science to create machines, processes, or structures. Whereas the starting point in science generally involves trying to explain or predict phenomena through the development and verification of theories and models, engineering is the process of physically achieving a goal by applying scientific ideas and theories in a practical way.

What do engineers do?

Although we tend to classify engineers and engineering courses under different headings, there is a good deal of overlap, and most engineering projects or processes require the input of many different types of engineer. When you look in more detail at the course content of different engineering programmes, you will see that there are many common elements to these. For instance, mechanical engineers will spend time studying electronic and electrical engineering as machines often use electricity as a power source; and civil engineering requires an understanding of the properties of materials, as does structural engineering.

Mechanical engineers

Mechanical engineers work in the development and manufacture of machines. This is obviously a very broad description: the word 'machine' covers an enormous range of devices, from medical equipment that is used to perform microsurgery through to aircraft carriers. Mechanical engineering courses include a number of specialist areas, such as aeronautical engineering and automotive engineering.

Electrical and electronic engineers

Electrical and electronic engineers work with electrical and electronic devices. As with mechanical engineering, these range from a microscopic scale (integrated circuits or solid state devices, for example) through to national electricity networks. Many universities offer a joint electrical/electronic engineering course, but it is also possible to specialise in just one of these subjects. There are close links between electronic engineering and computer or information technology (IT) engineering.

Information systems engineers

Information systems engineering is closely linked to electronic engineering. It focuses on computer systems and the transfer of electronic and digital information – mobile phones, the internet, and computer operating systems.

Civil engineers

Civil engineering deals with the large-scale infrastructure that is an essential part of daily life, such as roads, bridges, dams, water supplies, and office and apartment blocks. (The name civil engineering came about in order to differentiate projects that were there to benefit society in general from military engineering projects.)

Structural engineers

Structural engineering deals with the use and suitability of materials that are intended for creating structures such as buildings, bridges, sporting facilities, and electricity pylons. The discipline covers the structure and properties of materials on a microscopic level, and the behaviour of structures on a macroscopic scale. Structural engineers work closely with civil engineers and with architects. For example, once an architect has come up with a design for a new office block, structural engineers look at what materials will be required to ensure the project is feasible, before handing it over to the civil engineers to build it.

Materials engineers

Material engineering is closely related to structural engineering in that it looks at the properties of materials that are necessary to create structures. However, it also covers the use of materials for other requirements, such as plastics, ceramics, glass, polymers. A mobile phone manufacturer, for example, may work with materials engineers to ensure that the phone is strong enough to withstand daily knocks while at the same time being light and attractive.

Chemical engineers

Chemical engineering deals with the industrial processes that produce, for example, drugs, food, and fuels. Chemical engineers are not only concerned with the chemical properties of the materials they are producing or developing, but also the economic and safety aspects of the projects. Chemical engineering links closely with bioengineering, biomedical engineering, and biotechnology.

Biomedical engineers

Biomedical engineering (along with biotechnology) looks at the engineering aspects of living things, often for medical purposes. This can range from working with living materials, such as animal tissue, to the development of medical instrumentation (medical scanners, equipment used in surgery), and the design of machines and devices such as heart pacemakers and artificial limbs.

Petroleum engineers

Petroleum engineering covers all aspects of the oil, gas, and petroleum industries – from exploration and excavation, through refining and purification, to distribution. It covers geological studies, the chemical properties of hydrocarbons, and industrial processes.

Design and product engineers

Design and production engineering deals with the process of creating and developing systems and devices. As well as looking at production processes, such as the design of production lines and factories, design and product engineers have to be aware of safety and cost issues. As an example, take a new car, the production of which involves mechanical and electrical engineering input, computer hardware and software development, the choice of the right materials to ensure that the car will be safe, functional and attractive, and the creation of a production line that will be both efficient and cost-effective.

There are many other classifications of engineering disciplines and courses (see p. 17), and there are subsets of some of the areas mentioned above and courses that combine two or more of these disciplines. So, you will need to spend some time researching possible courses before deciding what you want to do. Advice on this can be found in Chapter 1.

Most engineering projects involve the input of a range of specialisms (see Figures 1 and 2).

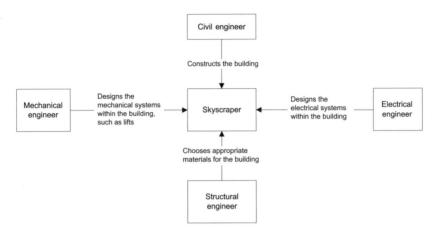

Figure 1: Input into building a skyscraper

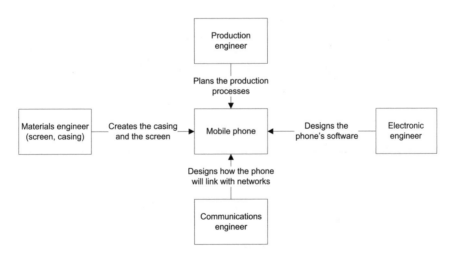

Figure 2: Input into building a mobile phone

Opportunities for engineers

Very few careers provide as many opportunities as engineering while at the same time offering secure employment prospects.

- Engineers can work anywhere in the world.
- The work can be theoretical or practical, and can be carried out within an office or on-site.
- Engineers can work for multinational companies or set up their own business.
- Engineers can work on any scale, from nanotechnology and micro-electronics, through to building the world's biggest structures.

Case studies

The Royal Academy of Engineering has launched a campaign, 'Shape the Future', which is aimed at students who are thinking about a career in engineering. As part of this campaign, the organisation has produced a series of case studies, which are essential reading for anyone contemplating studying engineering. You can access the booklet at the academy's website (www.raeng.org.uk/education/stf/pdf/tsz_fok_booklet.pdf). Two examples from this booklet are given in Chapter 7.

The Institution of Mechanical Engineers also publishes case histories on its website (see www.imeche.org).

Working internationally

Few careers provide greater opportunities to work or study overseas, and this is one of the attractions of engineering. Many of the world's major engineering projects are undertaken by multinational companies, and many engineers work freelance, choosing their projects and locations to suit their skills and circumstances. The rapid technological advances of the BRIC nations (Brazil, Russia, India, China) have created enormous demands for qualified engineers. In November 2010, for example, India reported a shortage of engineers, and is looking overseas for suitably qualified graduates to work on the country's infrastructure needs.

Case study

From Plymouth to paddy fields

'Graduating with a degree in civil engineering from Plymouth in 1980, I returned to the north of England to continue my training toward the institution professional examination. My company of choice was an engineering consultancy with a long pedigree in the design, project management, and supervision of power station construction. Based in Manchester, the next 10 years provided formative experience in major projects around the globe, including power stations in the UK, Isle of Man, Ireland, Greece, and India; coastal protection works and desalination plants in the Middle East; and roads, bridges, harbour, and jetty design in the UK. This included three years of on-site construction supervision of highway and power station projects.

The following six years provided opportunity to work with a number of renowned UK-based consulting engineers while specialising in the design of bridge works and other major highway structures. In 1996 I was given my first opportunity to work overseas. This was for a small Australian consulting service in Oman, responsible for projects ranging from highway feasibility studies in Pakistan to design and construction of the local Hyatt Hotel and the Royal Sports Stadium. The following years provided further opportunities to practice in my chosen fields of bridge, marine and power station engineering, including project management of the Incheon Bridge in South Korea, the sixth largest cable-stayed span in the world.

My current role is in Vietnam, helping to develop the country's infrastructure in terms of new power station design and construction. As the lead civil owner's engineer, my team is responsible for the design and construction review of a 1,200MW power station in rural Vietnam.'

Nigel Brook BSc CEng MICE

1 | Choosing your course

What to consider

You are allowed five choices on the UCAS application. The basic factors to consider when choosing your degree course are:

- the engineering course you are looking for
- where you want to study
- the kind of university you are aiming for
- your academic ability.

You need to think seriously about your choice of universities, as the decisions you will take now may determine your future career options. At this stage, you may already have an idea of which universities you want to consider, based on the advice of friends and/or family. But you need to be as open-minded as possible: make a list of between 10 and 20 universities in which you are interested. It's then important to reduce this to a much shorter list, and you can do this by researching each university in the listed below ways. This will give you a good feel for each institution as you go.

- Get hold of the prospectuses (both official and alternative) and departmental brochures (if they exist) for more details. Remember that university publications are there to attract applicants as well as to provide information, and may be selective about the information they provide, so read all of it bearing this in mind.
- Visit the websites of the universities you are considering. This is the best place to look for the most current information about a university. Another useful element to university websites is information on past and present students from a range of disciplines who give their views on student life at the institution. Some university websites even have email links to current students who can answer any questions that you may have.
- Go to university open days, if you can, and talk to former or current students. This will give you a feel for the place and you can decide if you would be happy to spend three or four years living there.
- Think about the realities of living there for at least three years – do you prefer to be in the centre of a city or on a campus, near your home or somewhere else in the UK?

- Discuss engineering and studying it as a subject with people you know who work as, or with, engineers; ask for their views on the reputations of different universities and courses. This may bring up some highly rated engineering institutions you may not have thought of.
- Investigate the grade requirements (be realistic about the grades you are expecting – your teachers at school or college will be able to advise you on this).
- Check that the course allows you to choose the particular options in which you are interested. If you are considering, for example, mechanical engineering but have a particular interest in aeronautics or automotive engineering, make sure that these options are available. You will not always know what each option actually covers by its title, so read the department's own prospectus carefully and address any unanswered questions by contacting the admissions tutors directly.
- Think about whether you would like your course to include an industrial placement. This can give you extremely valuable experience and is a great opportunity to make useful contacts for the future. Employers also like graduates who have had a practical placement. If you do choose such a course, it is well worth your while checking whose responsibility it will be to find you a placement. Does the university have a placement officer who will help you with this process, or is it entirely up to you to find something?
- Consider whether you want to spend some time abroad. If you are doing a course that has some foreign language content, it may be possible to do a work placement in that country. This could be particularly valuable as not only would you gain practical work experience, but you would also improve your language skills, which could give you the edge when you come to look for a job after you graduate. Engineers have more opportunities to work anywhere in the world than most other careers.
- Investigate how much practical or laboratory work is included in the course, and what are the practical engineering facilities. Find out whether the facilities include state-of-the-art machinery or testing equipment.
- Look at what IT facilities are offered. If you do not have your own laptop, will the university have facilities for you to manage without one of your own? Access to computing facilities can be very important when you are rushing to finish an important project report. You should also check how readily available are the books that you will be requiring for the course. Remember, university textbooks can be very expensive to buy.
- Look up the specialities of the engineering course staff. Are they experts in the field of engineering in which you are particularly interested? Use the internet to find out what their experience is and what they have published, as this will give you a better indication of a department's strengths.

Engineering courses

The structure of an engineering course will not only vary from discipline to discipline, but also from university to university. The common elements to all engineering courses are:

- mathematics (see p. 13)
- physical laws (for example Newton's laws or the laws of energy conservation or thermodynamics)
- the physics of materials (physical, electrical, and thermal properties)
- environmental, safety, and health issues
- cost and other economic issues.

Look at the course content in detail on the university websites, to ensure that your interests are covered. Two examples of the range of topics covered as part of an engineering degree are shown in the following boxes. The first gives the programme structure of the civil engineering course at Bristol University.

Civil Engineering at Bristol University

Year 1

Engineering mathematics
Properties of materials
Structural engineering
Geotechnics
Fluid mechanics
Civil engineering systems
Civil engineering design
Computing
Surveying
One from: thermodynamics; language

Year 2

Engineering mathematics
Properties of materials
Structural engineering
Geotechnics
Hydraulics
Civil engineering systems
Professional studies
Civil engineering design
One from: engineering architecture; computer modelling; language for specific purposes

---

Year 3

Structural engineering
Geotechnics
Water engineering
Civil engineering systems
Professional studies
Water resources project
Scheme design
Research project
Plus two third-year options from: engineering for the built environment, seismic analysis, timber engineering, open units

Source: www.bristol.ac.uk

The second box shows the programme structure of the University College London (UCL) electronic and electrical engineering course.

Electronic and electrical engineering at UCL

Year 1

Electronic circuits 1
Circuit analysis and synthesis 1
Digital circuits
Object-orientated programming 1
Electromagnetics
Mathematics for electronic engineers 1
Communications systems 1
Lab and design course: electronic
Engineering design principles
Optoelectronics 1

Year 2

Circuit analysis and synthesis 2
Optoelectronics 2
Fields and waves in electronic systems
Digital IC design
Semiconductor devices
Object-orientated programming 2
Mathematics for electronic engineers 2

> **Year 3**
>
> Project 1
> Further courses from a selection of options
> Students taking the International Programme spend the year at an approved university abroad
>
> Source: www.ucl.ac.uk

The importance of mathematics

All engineers use mathematical methods as an integral part of their work. While much of engineering relies on physical processes to develop and produce devices, machines, structures, fuels, or chemicals, these are all underpinned by mathematical calculations and models. If you look at the course outlines for engineering degree courses you will notice that a significant amount of the first-year course content involves mathematics. Also, most universities will specify an A level (or equivalent) mathematics grade in their entrance requirements. If you are interested in becoming an engineer you will need to study mathematics. If you want to be involved in production or design but do not want to study mathematics, you could look at alternative courses such as product design.

Very few universities require students to have A level further mathematics or the equivalent in order to be considered for engineering courses.

League tables

Newspapers often feature university rankings or league tables but there is no official ranking of universities or university courses in the UK, and so these tables are created using criteria selected by the newspapers themselves. There is a significant amount of variation between these tables, because each table will score the universities in a different way. So, you should approach these rankings with caution. However, they can be a useful aid to the selection process, particularly if you look at how the rankings are assessed rather than simply looking at a university's position in the tables. There will be some criteria that you might regard as being important to you – graduate job prospects, for example, while you might not be so interested in the student:teacher ratios.

The list on the following page shows the *Guardian* newspaper's (www.guardian.co.uk/education/universityguide) ranking of the top 10 universities in the UK in 2011 (© Guardian News & Media Ltd 2010).

1 Oxford
2 Cambridge
3 Warwick
4 St Andrews
5 UCL
6 Lancaster
7 Imperial
8 LSE
9= Loughborough
9= York

The list below shows the *Guardian* 2011 rankings for general engineering courses (© Guardian News & Media Ltd 2010).

1 Cambridge
2 Oxford
3 Bournemouth
4 Imperial
5 Leicester
6 Brunel
7 Warwick
8 Exeter
9 Durham
10 Lancaster

The list below shows the *Guardian* 2011 rankings for civil engineering courses (© Guardian News & Media Ltd 2010).

1 Imperial
2 Bristol
3 Sheffield
4 UCL
5 East London
6 Queen's Belfast
7 Bath
8 Heriot-Watt
9 Loughborough
10 Dundee

These rankings include a number of areas of assessment, some of which may not be relevant to you. The *Guardian* rankings can be re-ordered on the website by clicking on the category that you think is most important. For example, the list at the top of page 15 gives the engineering ranking ordered by entrance grades of students being accepted onto the course (which is a good indication of the quality of the students, © Guardian News & Media Ltd 2010).

1 Cambridge
2 Oxford
3 Durham
4 Imperial
5 Warwick
6 Brunel
7 Exeter
8 Leicester
9 Lancaster
10 Aberdeen

We could also look, for example, at the ranking by job prospects, based on destinations of graduates six months after graduating (see the list below, © Guardian News & Media Ltd 2010).

1 Oxford
2 Cambridge
3 Aberdeen
4 Bournemouth
5 Warwick
6 Leicester
7 Exeter
8 Edinburgh Napier
9 Brunel
10 Sheffield Hallam

After completing your research, you should be in a position to be able to narrow down your original list to the five choices for your UCAS form. Once you have done this, discuss the list with your teachers to see whether they think it includes sensible choices. They may ask you to think again about some of the choices. Common areas of concern for teachers are:

- all of the universities require the same entrance grades, which makes choosing an insurance offer (see p. 75) difficult
- the grade requirements are either too high (or too low) for the applicant's likely academic achievements
- there is too much variation within the choice of courses to enable the applicant to write a coherent and focused personal statement (see p. 34).

Entrance examinations

If you are applying to Cambridge University you will have to sit an extra entrance examination, the Thinking Skills Assessment (TSA).

TSA Cambridge

The information below is taken from the specimen papers available on the Cambridge Assessment website (www.admissionstests. cambridgeassessment.org.uk). Reprinted by permission of the University of Cambridge Local Examinations Syndicate.

- This test is taken at the interview.
- It consists of 50 questions to be completed in 90 minutes.
- Details can be found at the website listed above.

The TSA is available as an online or paper-based test. The college to which you are applying will specify which version you will take.

Sample test question

Every motorist pays the same amount for road tax, regardless of how much they use the roads: someone who covers as little as 1,000 miles pays the same as someone who covers 20,000. This is unfair. Road tax should be scrapped and the money raised by an increase in the tax on car fuel. Making this change would ensure that those who use the roads more would pay more. This would not only be a fairer system, but could also bring in more revenue.

Which of the following best illustrates the principle underlying the argument above?

A   People should receive free medical treatment only if they cannot afford to pay for it.
B   People who travel to work every day by train should pay a lower fare than those who travel only occasionally.
C   People who earn more than double the average wage should be made to pay much higher charges for dental treatment.
D   Television channels should be paid for by subscription so that only those people who watch them should be made to pay.
E   Telephone charges should be higher for business customers than for domestic customers because they are using the system only to make money.

Choosing the right course

Most universities will offer a wide range of engineering courses, and it is important for you to investigate these thoroughly before making your choices. A particular university might list the following on the UCAS website.

- Aeronautical engineering
- Aeronautical engineering with a year abroad
- Biomedical engineering
- Biomedical engineering with a year abroad
- Chemical engineering
- Chemical engineering with a year abroad
- Chemical with nuclear engineering
- Civil engineering
- Civil engineering with a year abroad
- Electrical and electronic engineering
- Electrical and electronic engineering with a year abroad
- Electrical and electronic engineering with management
- Information systems engineering
- Materials science and engineering
- Mechanical engineering
- Mechanical engineering with a year abroad
- Structural engineering

A broad outline of these courses can be found on page 3, but see the university website and prospectus for more details. You will need to spend some time going through these.

When considering possible courses, read through *all* of the course content. Do not just choose a course because of its title. Courses with the same name at different universities can vary immensely in their content, and within the courses themselves the likelihood is that you will have a range of options to choose from once you start your course. This is also important if you are interviewed (see Chapter 4) because you may be asked to justify your choice. Being able to discuss the course structure in detail will be an important factor in convincing the interviewer that you are a serious applicant.

Similar-sounding courses also do not always have the same entrance requirements (examination results and preferred A level subjects). Examination results are either specified as grade requirements (for example AAB) or tariff points (for example 300 – see Chapter 6). Unless you are applying post-results (as a mature applicant or during your gap year), your referee will be asked to predict the grades that you are expected to achieve in your examinations. You should find out in advance what he or she is going to predict, because this will determine your choice of universities and courses. For example, if you apply for five university courses that require AAB but your A level predictions are BBB, there will be a high chance of being rejected by all of your choices. You will then have try to find alternatives through the UCAS Extra scheme, or through Clearing (see Chapter 2). Similarly, if you are predicted to achieve A*AA, you are probably aiming too low if all of the courses you are applying for require CCC at A level.

As a rough guide, if you are predicted, say, ABB, you might want to choose one course that requires AAB, three that require ABB, and one that requires BBB. This means that you not only have a good chance of getting a number of offers but it also gives you options if you do not quite meet the grade requirements (see Chapter 6).

Placements and overseas study

Studying abroad and/or completing a work placement could also be factors that affect your degree selection. It is possible to study engineering in many countries as part of a degree based at a British university. Not all of these courses send you off for a full year though: there are schemes that only last for one term or semester. You do not need to be a linguist either, as it is always possible to study overseas in an English-speaking location such as North America, South Africa, Australia, or Malaysia.

The availability of student exchanges has increased through programmes such as Erasmus, which encourage universities to provide international opportunities where practical – particularly in Europe. The popularity of overseas study has encouraged some universities to develop special exchange relationships with universities further afield.

Methods of assessment and study

To obtain your degree, you will need to undertake a combination of examinations (normally spread over two or three years) and coursework, although individual units may be assessed purely by coursework or dissertation. Methods of studying, such as lectures, seminars, tutorials, practicals, workshops, and self-study, tend not to vary much between universities (except for Oxford and Cambridge, where they centre around the one-to-one tutorial system). Some institutions, however, do offer part-time courses and even distance learning for a few degrees.

Combined honours courses

There are a number of joint or combined honours degrees available, but there is less flexibility with engineering courses than there might be with arts or humanities subjects. This is simply because engineering degrees tend to lead towards careers in engineering, and so they focus on this.

However, many engineers end up running their own engineering company or business, or taking a managerial role within an engineering firm, and so a wide range of degrees that combine engineering with management are available.

As an example, we will look at the MEng Electrical and Electronic Engineering with Management course at Imperial College, London.

MEng course elements, Imperial College, London

Year 1

- Analogue electronics
- Analysis of circuits
- Digital electronics
- Energy conversion
- Introduction to signals and communications
- Mathematics
- Semiconductor physics
- Software engineering
- Professional development
- Weekly laboratory practicals (electronics and computing)

Year 2

- Algorithms and data structures
- Analogue electronics
- Communications
- Control engineering
- Digital electronics
- Electrical power engineering
- Fields and devices
- Introduction to computer architecture
- Mathematics
- Signals and non-linear systems
- Technical communication
- A non-technical subject
- Weekly laboratory practicals (electronics and computing)

Year 3

You must take a minimum of eight and a maximum of nine modules, which includes three core business courses.

Year 4 (MEng)

This year consists of a wide range of advanced technical modules. A substantial individual project (40% of the final year mark) is undertaken, and project work starts in the first term and continues throughout the year.

Source: www.imperial.ac.uk

You will notice that the programme for the first two years of the MEng course at Imperial College concentrates on the theoretical and technical aspects of electrical and electronic engineering. In the third and fourth years (four, because this is an MEng, not a BEng course, see p. 85) there is more flexibility for you to steer the degree towards your own interests, and you would study business courses alongside the engineering courses.

If you intend to apply for a joint or combined honours course, you must ensure that your personal statement addresses both aspects of the course (see p. 34).

Other courses

Foundation degrees

Foundation degrees are two-year full time (or three-year part time or distance learning) courses, which are provided by some universities. (Do not confuse these with the foundation courses offered to some international students in place of A levels or the equivalent.) They are intended for students who do not have conventional academic backgrounds, for example students who left school after taking their GCSEs and have been working in a relevant field, or mature applicants. Many employers will accept Foundation degrees as an acceptable qualification; and there are many opportunities for students with a Foundation degree to follow this with an extra year of university study to gain a bachelor's degree. You can apply for Foundation degrees through UCAS (www.ucas.com). Subjects available at Foundation degree level include all the major engineering fields, and some specialist ones (such as Northampton University's lift engineering course, which is a three-year distance learning course).

Higher national diplomas

Higher national diplomas (HNDs) are usually two-year courses, often equivalent to, or taught simultaneously with, the first two years of a bachelor's degree. Students who are successful on the HND course can study for a third year to gain a bachelor's degree. Entrance requirements are normally less stringent. For example, Coventry University asks for 220 UCAS tariff points from three A levels (including A level mathematics and/or physics for entrance onto a degree-level course, but only 160 points from two A levels, with no subject requirements, for the HND course).

Academic and career-related factors

Academic ability

It is important to be honest about what you think you will achieve in your A levels or equivalent because for most, this is the deciding factor for selection. The best way to get a strong sense of your predicted results it to speak to your teachers.

Remember, be realistic; do not think too pessimistically about what you hope to achieve, but on the other hand do not deceive yourself that you will miraculously gain much higher grades than you are predicted. So, for example, if you are predicted to get BBB (which amounts to 3×100 = 300 points), then any combination which produces 300 points (i.e. ABC or AAD) may be acceptable. However, you should not assume this.

For more details about UCAS and filling in your applications, see *How to Complete Your UCAS Application, 2012 entry*.

Educational facilities

Take a look the facilities the university has to offer. Here is a checklist of what to look out for:

- access to lecturers if you need help
- computer facilities
- course materials
- laboratory provision
- lecture theatres
- library facilities
- multi-media facilities
- study facilities.

Quality of teaching

The Higher Education Funding Council for England, the Higher Education Funding Council for Wales, the Scottish Funding Council and the Department for Education and Learning of Northern Ireland assess the level of teaching across the UK. Their findings are publicly available – see www.hefce.ac.uk, www.hefcw.ac.uk, www.sfc.ac.uk and www.delni.gov.uk. League tables (see p. 11) normally incorporate these into their rankings.

Type of institution

There are three types of institution from which you can obtain a degree.

1. 'Old' universities
2. 'New' universities
3. Higher education colleges

The 'old' universities

Traditionally seen as the more academic universities (Oxford, Cambridge, and St Andrews to name a few), usually with higher admission requirements, the old universities are well established with good libraries and research facilities. They have a reputation for being resistant to change, but most have introduced modern elements into their degrees such as modular courses, an academic year split into two semesters and programmes such as Erasmus.

The 'new' universities

Pre-1992 these were polytechnics, institutes, or colleges, for example Kingston, Central Lancashire, and Westminster. They form a separate group today because they tend to still hold true to the original polytechnic mission of vocational courses and strong ties with industry, typically through placements and work experience. Because of this there are a number of excellent engineering degree courses at new universities, which are very well regarded and highly competitive to get into. Some are still looked down upon by certain employers because of their generally lower academic entry requirements. But the 'new' universities have a good name for flexible admissions and learning, modern approaches to their degrees and good pastoral care.

Colleges of higher education

These are specialist institutions which provide excellent facilities in their chosen fields, despite their size. They are sometimes affiliated to universities. This form of franchising means the college buys the right to teach the degree, which the university will award, provided that the course meets the standards set by the university.

Non-academic considerations

Finances

Finance is an important factor to consider, as you will need to juggle a lot of outgoings when you go to university. You will need to take into account:

- accommodation costs
- availability of part-time work in the area to earn some extra money
- living costs, such as food
- travel from your accommodation to the university during term time
- travel from your home to and from the university for holidays
- proximity to your home, family, and friends; will it cost you a lot of money to visit friends or to go home?

Accommodation

Accommodation can vary wildly between institutions so you will need to think about where you would feel most comfortable. Do you want to live in halls of residence with other students, or in private housing? Do you want to be near your lectures or are you happy to live further away from the university?

Most institutions have an accommodation officer who will help you find a suitable place to live. Many universities guarantee a room in halls of residence to first-year students. But you will probably have to fend for yourself at some stage, so check on the availability of student housing.

Entertainment

You will be spending the next few years in a new place so you will need to have a look at the entertainment facilities it has to offer both within and outside the university. Are your particular interests or hobbies catered for? If you're a keen sports enthusiast, have a look at the facilities on offer and the sorts of clubs and teams you can join.

Site and size

- Campus university outside of a town or city?
- Campus within a town or city?
- University buildings at various locations within a town or city?
- Large or small?

While some students have a clear picture of where they want to study, others are fairly geographically mobile, preferring instead to concentrate on choosing the right degree course and see where they end up. But university life is not going to be solely about academic study. It is truly a growing experience – educationally, socially, culturally – and, besides, three or four years can really drag if you are not happy outside the lecture theatre.

Sources of finance

There has been significant news coverage in recent years about the funding of university courses. In the 1970s and 1980s, university education was effectively free for UK students, and most students were given maintenance grants to cover living costs in addition to having their fees paid. The situation at the time of writing this book is that students pay a contribution towards the cost of their courses (see below) and can take out student loans to cover living costs. But in late 2010, the UK government published a report (the Browne report) on student funding which recommended changes to the system – in particular, raising the cap on the contribution paid by students and the introduction of a new system of recovering the money through taxes. See the UCAS website's finance pages for the latest information.

The latest figures show that average graduate debt is around £5,600 per year of study. This varies from an average of £6,400 per year for students studying in Wales, down to £2,600 per year in Scotland. In August 2010, the BBC reported that total debts could rise to an average of 'up to £25,000' for students starting courses in 2010.

Currently, all UK and EU students pay tuition fees of up to £3,290 per year (2010 entry) as a contribution towards the cost of the course, but this will almost certainly increase significantly in future years. Some students will have up to 100% of this paid by their local authority, depending on the income of their parents. For details of how these grants are calculated, see the Directgov website (www.direct.gov.uk). Even if you are not eligible for a grant, your fees may not have to be paid while you are studying – you can take out a loan for which repayments are not compulsory until you are working and earning more than £15,000 per year. The repayment of the loan is calculated as a percentage of your earnings over the £15,000 threshold, and so the more you earn, the quicker the loan will be repaid. In previous years, it was possible to take a 'repayment holiday', which allowed students to stop making payments for a short period, but this has been discontinued.

Scottish students who choose a Scottish university do not pay any tuition fees (although this may change in the future). There are a number of grants available for students in Scotland, including a Young Students' Bursary of up to £2,640 per year, and the Independent Students' Bursary of up to £1,000 a year. Details can be found at www.student-support-saas.gov.uk. Welsh students studying in Scotland pay reduced fees.

Welsh students studying in Wales are charged up to £3,290 a year, but can receive a grant to offset the fees. There are also grants available from the Welsh Assembly (Assembly Learning Grants – ALG) for up to £5,067 per year, and a bursary scheme operated by the Welsh universities. For details, see www.studentfinancewales.co.uk.

The UCAS website (www.ucas.com) has full details of fees and support arrangements.

Engineering students are more fortunate than their peers who are studying other subjects, because of the large number of sponsorship and bursary schemes available from engineering institutes, companies and the universities themselves. This is because it is recognised that the UK needs to attract more able students into engineering. The starting points for this are:

- the university engineering departments
- the engineering institutes (contact details are given at the end of this book).

The engineering institutes or institutions are professional bodies that accredit and represent their members, provide training and information, promote their particular fields of engineering, organise or offer scholarships and help engineers with their careers.

The level of sponsorship varies from course to course, university to university, and institute to institute; and also changes from year to year. You will need to spend some time researching your options.

Sponsorship can include:

- financial aid during the degree course
- paid or part-funded work placements during holidays or a gap year
- work or study placements overseas
- improved chances of jobs with the sponsoring companies after graduation.

Several publications giving details of funds and bursaries offered by educational trusts are available, including the *Education Trust Directory of Grant-making Trusts* published by the Charities Aid Foundation. You should also refer to the Education Grants Advisory Service (www.egas-online.org).

The professional engineering institutes also offer some scholarships.

Examples of engineering scholarships

Imperial College scholarships for engineering students

Tallow Chandlers scholarship

This is awarded annually to one home undergraduate student from a financially disadvantaged background studying within the Department of Earth Sciences and Engineering in the Faculty of Engineering. The scholarships will provide £5,000 per annum for a maximum of four years, subject to satisfactory progress.

City & Guilds scholarship

The City & Guilds scholarship is awarded annually to two home undergraduates from financially disadvantaged backgrounds studying within the Faculty of Engineering. The scholarships will each provide £2,500 per annum for a maximum of four years, subject to satisfactory progress.

Holligrave Scholarship

Founded from funds donated by the Cloth Workers' Foundation, one award is made annually to an engineering undergraduate from a financially disadvantaged background. The award is worth £1,500 in your first year of study and £1,000 each year thereafter. The award is payable for a maximum of four years, subject to satisfactory progress.

Source: www.imperial.ac.uk

Bath University scholarships for engineering students

- Eliahou Dangoor Scholarships (for science, technology, engineering and mathematics)
- Hertzian Fund Scholarship (for electronic and electrical engineering)
- Jeremy Fry Memorial Scholarship in Engineering
- John Barr Scholarships (for MEng or BEng)
- Nick Wood Electrical Engineering Scholarship

Source: www.bath.ac.uk

Bristol University scholarships for engineering students

Some colleges not only offer scholarships to UK-home students, but also to international students. For example, at Bristol University, international students can apply for:

- Barry Thomas Scholarship in computer science
- Edmund Boulton Scholarships for engineering design and engineering mathematics

- Mechanical Engineering Scholarship
- Paul Dirac Scholarship in electrical and electronic engineering
- Roderick Collar Scholarship in aeronautical engineering
- Sir Alfred Pugsley Scholarship in civil engineering

Source: www.bristol.ac.uk

The Institution of Mechanical Engineers

'Undergraduate scholarships and grants offer assistance to students who are about to start or have already started on mechanical engineering degrees accredited by the Institution. [The] current Undergraduate Scholarship Scheme is sponsored by AMEC and Rolls–Royce plc. who are offering sponsorship to students to assist them with their accredited degree-level programmes.'

Undergraduate scholarship

These scholarships offer mechanical engineering undergraduates up to £4,000 for their studies.

Overseas study award

'These grants enable students to study or do work placements overseas as part of their degree programmes. Each overseas study award is worth up to £750.'

Group project award

'Group projects are often integral to undergraduate engineering degrees. Affiliate members of the Institution can receive financial assistance for their group projects. The award can enable groups to attend or participate in international conferences related to engineering, science and technology, which are relevant to their group project. Alternatively, the funds can enable groups to attend or take part in engineering, science and technology based projects or activities overseas, which are relevant to their group project.

'The group project award is worth £250 per individual in each group. The group is limited to a maximum of 8 members.'

Source: Institution of Mechanical Engineers, www.imeche.org

Suggested timescale

Use the timescale below to help you to plan your application.

Year 12

- Start to think about the sort of courses you might want to follow. Talk to your teachers, your family, and your friends.
- Find out about university open days and visit some universities.

June/July

- Make a shortlist of your courses.

August

- Get some copies of the official and alternative (student-written) prospectuses, and departmental brochures for extra detail. They can usually be found in school or college libraries, but all the information can also be found by looking at university websites.

Year 13

September

- Complete your application online and submit it to UCAS via a referee. It will be accepted from 1 September onwards.

15 October

- Deadline for applying for places at Oxford or Cambridge.

November

- Universities hold their open days and sometimes their interviews.
- Entrance examinations for some Oxford and Cambridge courses.

15 January

- Deadline for submitting your application to UCAS. (Late applications may be considered, but your chances are limited since some of the places will have already gone).

March/April

- Universities will have made their decisions and offers will be sent directly to you. If you are rejected by all of your choices, you can use UCAS Extra to look at other universities.
- Fill out yet more forms. This time they are for fees and student loans, which you can get from your school, college or local authority.

15 May

- You must tell UCAS which offer you have accepted firmly an. which one is your back-up. The deadline is two weeks after the final decision you receive if this falls earlier.

Summer

- Sit your exams and wait for your results. When the A level results are published, UCAS will get in touch and tell you whether your chosen universities have confirmed your conditional offers. Do not be too disappointed if you have not got in to your chosen institution; just get in touch with your school/college or careers office and wait until Clearing begins in mid-August, when all remaining places are filled. You will be sent instructions on Clearing automatically, but it is up to you to get hold of the published lists of available places and to contact the universities directly.
- If you have done better than expected, you can use the Adjustment system to look for universities that require higher grades.

2 | Completing your UCAS application

This chapter is designed to help you to complete your UCAS application, and in particular, to write a comprehensive and convincing personal statement. More specific advice on filling in your application is given in *How to Complete Your UCAS Application 2012 Entry*, which is updated annually.

Competition for places

While the ratio of applicants to places for engineering courses is lower than for many other subjects (see below), the competition for places at the higher ranked universities is intense. Thus many candidates, while being successful at gaining a place on an engineering degree course, do so either through Clearing or at one of their lower preference universities. You should aim as high as you can (within the boundaries set by your examination results and predictions) in terms of your choice of university, as employers will look not only at what you studied but where you studied. Therefore do all that you can to ensure that your choice of university will stand you in good stead in the future.

UCAS (www.ucas.com) reports that for 2009 entry, around 28,000 students applied for 25,000 places. Of these, approximately one in every nine applications were from women. International students were less successful in gaining places than their UK counterparts – 2,000 of the 2,700 EU applicants were successful, along with 5,000 of the 6,600 non-EU international students. The ratio of applicants to places varies from course to course. For example, the success rate for mechanical engineering applicants was around 80%, whereas 98% of electrical and electronic engineering applicants gained places.

As with most things in life, the more planning and preparation you do, the better your chances of success. This is, of course, true for your studies and examinations; but it is also the case that research and a well-planned UCAS application will give you a much better chance of being made offers by your chosen universities. This applies to all aspects of the application: choosing your courses and universities, looking at their entrance requirements, writing a personal statement that will demonstrate your seriousness about, and suitability for, the course, and ensuring that you are prepared for any interviews or entrance tests.

Ignore those who tell you that 'if you are lucky, you will get an offer' – if you pitch your applications at the level that is appropriate for your qualifications (past and predicted) and prepare properly, you can remove most of the uncertainty from your application. The next chapters will tell you how to do this.

The UCAS application

The UCAS application is completed online, via the UCAS website. There are five sections to complete.

1. **Personal information:** your name, address, nationality, how the course is going to be funded, how you wish UCAS to communicate with you. This should be the easiest part of the form to complete, but you need to read the instructions carefully to avoid making mistakes.
2. **Your choices of university and course:** you are allowed to choose five courses and, as you will see later in this chapter, you need to think carefully about this. Again, pay particular attention to the course codes and university codes, and ensure that all the required information (where you intend to live, which campus you are applying to) is included.
3. **Education:** examination results, where you have studied, examinations to be sat. This section requires particular care, and you will need to discuss this with your school or college to ensure that, for example, AS unit results are correctly entered.
4. **Employment:** if you have had gaps in your education because you were in employment, you need to give details here.
5. **Personal statement:** see p 34.

Once you have completed all of these sections, your referee will add his or her comments about your suitability for your chosen courses. This is normally done by someone at your school or college (such as a housemaster or head of sixth form) but for applicants who are not at school, this might be an employer (see Chapter 5).

University engineering departments are looking for motivated, well-qualified individuals, and so they are keen to provide as much encouragement and practical advice as possible. If you look hard enough, you will find lots of information from the universities which will help you with your application. As an example, see the excerpts from the admissions advice on the Bristol University website for MEng Engineering Mathematics applicants in the box across the page.

Advice on the UCAS application process

'Candidates who are invited to attend a departmental Admissions Day are required to do so as an indicator of commitment to their chosen course. The Admissions Day includes an informal interview with an academic member of the department. Although primarily designed to establish that each candidate has applied to the appropriate course and whether the student's details have changed in any way since the original UCAS form was submitted, the interviewer will also look at other criteria, which may include, but are not limited to:

- demonstration of mathematical, analytical and technical skills
- evidence of clear thinking and understanding
- evidence of motivation and commitment
- interest in the subject
- non-academic achievement and/or experience
- responses to challenges faced.

'The interviewer does not make a selection decision. The informal interviews are used to determine the level of offer and to provide a more comprehensive picture of each candidate for the Admissions Team. Candidates who do not meet the minimum entry criteria, but for whom the course may be suitable, are invited to a formal interview as part of the Admissions Day. All interviews intended to select students are conducted by two people, including a member of staff with training in fair and effective recruitment techniques and are undertaken in accordance with the University's policy on equal opportunities.

'We take an holistic approach to all applications, ensuring that the educational and social context in which an applicant applies is taken into consideration, where supported by clear evidence that this may have adversely affected academic achievement.'

Personal Statement criteria

The information contained within each Personal Statement and School Reference is carefully considered for each applicant. Evidence of potential to complete the course may include, but is not restricted to:

- demonstration of interest in and commitment to mathematics and engineering
- strong mathematical, analytical and technical skills
- relevant reading, research or experience beyond the A level syllabus
- appropriateness of the chosen course to the candidate's interests and aspirations

- non-academic achievement and experience (for example work experience in industry)
- positions of responsibility, team working
- standard of written English.

Source: www.bristol.ac.uk

The personal statement

Arguably, the most important part of your UCAS application is the personal statement. It is also the one part of the form where you have complete freedom to decide how you wish to demonstrate your suitability for the course to the selectors. You have 4,000 characters (47 lines) to convince the five universities that you are applying to that:

- you have good reasons for studying engineering
- you have researched thoroughly about your future career
- you have appropriate personal and academic qualities to become a successful engineer
- you will be able to contribute something to the department and to the university.

Before you can write a personal statement you have to think carefully about your choice of courses. This is because each admissions tutor will read the personal statement with his or her own course in mind, and he/she will expect what you write to be consistent with the course. For this reason, make sure that the five courses you choose are closely linked in terms of course content and outcome. If you are applying for a civil engineering course, the selector will expect to read about your interest in civil engineering, books related to the subject that you have read, and relevant work experience. Similarly, an admissions tutor for electronic engineering will expect the personal statement to address this subject. Clearly, you cannot convince both that you are serious about their courses in one personal statement.

This is also true of joint honours courses which are usually read by selectors from both of the departments to which you are applying. If you want to apply for a joint honours engineering and management course, someone from the engineering faculty will expect to read about engineering while their colleagues from the management department will want to read about management. This is fine if you apply to five similar courses, but if you apply for, say, three engineering with management and two single honours engineering courses you will find it difficult to satisfy the selectors from the two different types of course.

The UCAS system allows applicants to apply for more than one course at a particular university. But beware: applying for two courses at the same university does not double your chances of studying there. As an example, take the case of a student who is desperate to study at a particular university, perhaps because she has friends there or she likes the city. She decides to apply for both the civil engineering and bio-medical engineering courses. The admissions tutor for civil engineering will look at her application for the civil engineering course, and the admissions tutor for biomedical engineering will look at the application for this course.

Our applicant's main interest is civil engineering, so her personal state-ment emphasises this, but it also devotes one paragraph to her interest in biomedical issues. The civil engineering admissions tutor reading the personal statement will judge it on how it addresses this course, so he/she might not be fully convinced that the student is serious because the personal statement will not focus enough on the reasons for the choice of civil engineering, and what the candidate has done to investi-gate it (reading, work experience, etc.). Similarly, biomedical engi-neering is a very specialist area, and the admissions tutor for this course will expect to read a personal statement that focuses on this, and he/she is not going to be very interested in reading about bridges and roads.

So, by trying to give herself a better chance of getting to this university, the applicant is actually reducing her chances. There are some instances where it is possible to apply for two separate courses at the same uni-versity, if they are very similar, but it would be advisable to discuss this with the university admissions department before doing so. So, when writing the personal statement, try to imagine how it will come across to each of the departments to which you are applying. Do not try to write something too general in order to allow yourself the luxury of applying to a wider range of courses.

Advice from an admissions tutor

'From a Personal Statement, we are looking for a well-rounded but focused and committed individual. Therefore, an indication that they can get their hands dirty (metaphorically speaking) over a long-term technical project is highly desirable. What we are not interested in are flowery quotes about the applicant wanting to solve the world's problems (often encouraged by parents and teachers). Our alarm bells also start ringing when an applicant has too many non-academic commitments, but equally no outside interests.'

Dr Stepan Lucyszyn, Undergraduate Admissions Tutor for the Department of Electrical and Electronic Engineering (EEE), at Imperial College London

The structure of the personal statement

What is a perfect personal statement? Of course, there is no such thing. The key to writing a personal statement is to think about the word 'personal' – it is about you and so it has to reflect your strengths, achievements, qualities, research and ambitions. Having said that, there are some elements that are important in creating a successful personal statement:

- why you have chosen the course
- how you have investigated whether the course is suitable for you
- what makes you stand out from your peers
- other information relevant to the application, for example if you are taking a gap year, what you will be doing during the year.

Why you have chosen the course

This could include:

- what first interested you in engineering, for example watching the news about a new engineering project, an article in a newspaper about new developments in the mobile phone industry, or personal experience such as work experience. It could date back many years, for example how you liked taking things apart and reassembling them when you were very young
- things you have studied at school, for example a topic in physics or chemistry that particularly interested you
- a combination of your particular interests and academic skills.

How you have investigated whether the course is suitable for you

This could include:

- books, periodicals or websites that you read
- work experience (see Chapter 3)
- lectures that you have attended
- skills that you have gained from your A levels.

What makes you stand out from your peers

This could include:

- academic achievements, for example prizes or awards
- extracurricular activities and achievements
- responsibilities, for example school prefect, head of house, captain of netball
- voluntary or charity work
- evidence of teamwork, for example sports teams, Duke of Edinburgh expeditions, part-time jobs
- travel.

Other information relevant to the application

This could include:

- gap year plans
- personal circumstances, for example it may be necessary for you to study in your home city because of the need to help to care for a disabled parent.

A sample personal statement

Character count (with spaces): 1,772

I first became interested in engineering during my AS physics classes (1). As a child I had always enjoyed taking things apart, although I was not always able to put them back together again.

To further investigate engineering, I spent a week at a local archi-tecture practice, looking at how they worked with a structural engineer to ensure that their designs were practical. I also visited a construction project as part of my school's work experience programme, and I was fascinated to see how things I had read about and studied were used in real life (2). I have also read as much as I can about engineering, including 'A Short History of Engineering Materials' by John Cameron (3). I have enjoyed going to public lectures on engineering, and talking to engineers, who have given me a much better idea about a career as an engi-neer (4).

Alongside physics, I am studying mathematics and history of art. Mathematics is an important tool for engineers (5), as well as teaching me to think in a logical way. History of art is an analytical subject, and it puts architecture within a social and political con-text. It also involves looking at the use of materials, and how architecture and sculpture were able to develop as new materials were introduced (6).

I enjoy sport and music. I am captain of my school football team and so have had to develop leadership and communication skills as well as physical fitness. I play the guitar in a band, and the cello in the school orchestra, which help me with my manual dexterity and teamwork. Outside of school, I enjoy cooking and cycling. I am a member of my local cycling club and compete most weekends.

I believe that my combination of A levels and my research into engineering as a career make engineering an ideal choice for me.

Points raised by this personal statement

An admissions tutor who read this sample personal statement made the following points.

General

Whilst it is clear that the candidate has done some research, there is very little detail in the statement – it is very general – and so I do not really get a clear picture of the depth of knowledge the candidate has about engineering, or about his/her particular areas of interest. It is also, to be honest, a little on the bland side and also a bit frustrating – a lot of sentences which should lead to something that will interest me end without giving me any information.

Specific points (the numbers refer to the relevant passages in the statement)

1. It would have been nice if he/she could have given an example – perhaps it was electricity, or the behaviour of materials, or some problems involving forces?
2. This should have been the most interesting part of the statement. The candidate could have told me about the links between his/her studies and the work experience. This will tell me that the student has gained something from the work experience, and that he/she is thinking about engineering rather than just doing work experience to look good on the application form.
3. I am always encouraged when students read around the subject, but what I would like to know is, again, some detail. How do the ideas in the book link to A level study and the real world?
4. This would have been an ideal opportunity for the candidate to show me that he/she has been really thinking hard about his/her future career and about whether he/she has the right qualities to be a successful engineer.
5. Give an example.
6. Not many applicants for engineering study history of art, so this immediately makes him/her stand out. And I don't know much about history of art, so an example here would be interesting for me to learn about – I'm sure it would make me want to learn more by meeting the candidate.

A revised (and much better) version of the personal statement, based on the above advice, is now given.

Revised sample personal statement

Character count (with spaces): 3,074

As a child I had always enjoyed taking things apart, although I was not always able to put them back together again. I first became seriously interested in engineering during my AS physics classes when we looked at the properties of solid materials, and I began to understand why, for example, the development of reinforced concrete revolutionised the construction industry.

To further investigate engineering, I spent a week at a local architecture practice, looking at how they worked with a structural engineer to ensure that their designs were practical. I also visited a construction project as part of my school's work experience programme, and I was fascinated to see how things I had read about and studied were used in real life. The engineers explained that the concrete girders used to hang the curtain walls of the office block had to be strengthened along their top surfaces because in a cantilever, the tensile forces are at the top and concrete is weaker in tension than it is in compression. I have also read as much as I can about engineering, including 'A Short History of Engineering Materials' by John Cameron and I was fascinated about how the use of cast iron in early 20th-century America enabled architects and engineers to build the prototypes to today's skyscrapers. I have enjoyed going to public lectures on engineering, and talking to engineers, who have given me a much better idea about a career as an engineer. In particular, I began to understand that an engineer needs to be able to analyse information quickly and to be able to solve problems. My aim is to study structural engineering and then to work alongside architects in the creation of exciting new buildings.

Alongside physics, I am studying mathematics and history of art. Mathematics is an important tool for engineers because the starting point of any engineering project is an analysis of its feasibility. The use of integration to find a centre of mass, for example, can help with the design of an asymmetric building. History of art is an analytical subject, and puts architecture within a social and political context. It also involves looking at the use of materials, and how architecture and sculpture were able to develop as new materials were introduced. The transition from the small, squat Romanesque churches to tall and graceful gothic cathedrals in Europe was due to the invention of the flying buttresses, which, in turn, were only effective when tensile forces were reduced by the addition of heavy statues or decorative stone elements were added.

I enjoy sport and music. I am captain of my school football team and so have had to develop leadership and communication skills as well as physical fitness. I play the guitar in a band, and the cello in the school orchestra, which help me with my manual dexterity and teamwork. Outside of school, I enjoy cooking and cycling. I am a member of my local cycling club and compete most weekends.

I believe that my combination of A levels and my research into engineering as a career make engineering an ideal choice for me.

Adding the extra information requested by this admissions tutor would add detail, make it more interesting for him to read (so he is more likely to want to meet the student), demonstrate that the student is interested enough in the subject to be thinking about links between his studies and what he has experienced, and bring it up to the required length.

Advice from an admissions tutor

'Apart from good predicted A level and English examination results, we are looking for signs that the applicant has the bandwidth to comfortably attain his or her academic goals and to also enjoy other pursuits; for example the ability to master another language, musical instrument, sport, or hobby and take them to ever greater levels of achievement.'

Stepan Lucyszyn, Undergraduate Admissions Tutor for the Department of Electrical and Electronic Engineering (EEE) at Imperial College London

Links and connections

A good way to show that you have thought about the subject and the course is to make links and connections between your different areas of research and preparation. You could think about linking:

- aspects of your A level subjects with things you will study on the course
- qualities necessary for success in this field with your own experiences (for example captaining a school team or organising a school event
- an article that you read on the internet and something that you observed in your work experience.

You could link:

- an article you read about the increasing storage capacity of computer memory with something you studied about semiconductors
- the design of a new building with your study of forces in physics
- the need for engineers to be good communicators with your role as your class representative at school
- the follow-up research you did on wind turbines with an on-site visit on a school trip
- a news story on a new aircraft design with an article in the *New Scientist* about composite materials.

How to get started on the personal statement

A good strategy is to start by making lists of anything that you think is relevant to your application. Then begin to organise them into sections. Your personal statement could include some of the following points.

My interest in the subject began because of:

- a newspaper article I read
- a book I read
- a news item
- my work experience
- my parents' work
- my A level subjects.

I have researched this subject by:

- reading books
- reading the *New Scientist*
- reading the Royal Academy of Engineering website
- work experience
- attending lectures
- talking to . . .
- downloading a podcast of a university lecture on iTunes U.

My work experience taught me:

- that the qualities a good engineer needs are . . .
- how to relate what I have been taught in A level physics to real-life situations
- the importance of teamwork/accuracy/decision making . . .

Other relevant points:

- my A level subjects are useful because . . .
- my Saturday job is useful because . . .
- my role as school prefect has taught me . . .
- being captain of the 1st XV has taught me . . . (or netball, or leader of the orchestra, or . . .)

- during my gap year I have arranged to . . .
- I was awarded first prize for . . .

Only when you have the ideas structured in some sort of logical order should you start to write full sentences and to link the points. On no account should your first steps towards writing a personal statement be to:

- plan how you are going to say all you want in exactly 47 lines.
- write down your ideas in perfectly formed sentences, suitable for the final version
- download sample personal statements from the internet and try to adapt them.

Language

It is important that you use succinct language in your personal statement and make every word count. Remember that you are limited on the number of characters you may use so it is important not to use up this vital space with superfluous language. Keep it as simple and clear as you can, rather than using overcomplicated language in an effort to impress.

For example:

'I was privileged to be able to undertake some work experience with a well-known engineering company where I was able to see the benefit of having the ability to be confident with information technology' – approximately 200 characters.

Could be rewritten as:

'My three weeks' work placement at Rolls-Royce showed me the importance of being proficient in using spreadsheets' – approximately 112 characters.

Similarly:

'I was honoured to be chosen to play the lead role in my most recent school drama production, and interacting with the producer and the rest of the cast involved a significant degree of communication and teamwork' – approximately 180 characters.

The last quote could be rewritten as:

'Performing as the lead in my school play taught me to work and communicate effectively with others' – approximately 100 characters.

Phrases to avoid

- 'I was honoured to be . . .'
- 'I was privileged to . . .'

- 'From an early age . . .'
- 'It has always been my dream to . . .'

Sample personal statements

These statements were written by students applying for engineering courses for 2011.

Please remember that these are *personal* statements, that is, they reflect the experiences and ambitions of the students who wrote them – so do not attempt to copy them or to adapt them for your own use.

Personal statement 1

Character count (with spaces): 3,719

I come to read engineering from an unusual position. Along with A level chemistry, maths, further maths and ancient history, I studied design and technology: resistant materials to AS level. It was in studying design that I became convinced that what I wanted to study further was engineering. I therefore decided to use my gap year to study A level physics, which I am enjoying very much, particularly because it connects so many of the topics I have already studied.

Design introduced me to the properties of materials, and how these properties affect their applications in building and manufacture. Learning about carbon fibre and its uses in Formula 1 cars was particularly interesting. Chemistry enabled me to understand the composition of these materials and their resultant properties such as the lubricating properties of graphite created by the layers of carbon atoms. I have particularly enjoyed the mechanics modules of my maths courses, and look forward to further developing the mathematical models I have studied.

To get more of an insight into engineering as a degree I went on a Headstart course last summer at the University of Surrey. I enjoyed the whole experience, particularly the sessions focusing on the manufacture, properties, uses and limitations of reinforced concrete, where I was able to draw on my knowledge of moments from my mechanics modules and tensile and compressive forces from design. These gave me an idea about what being a structural engineer involves, and the problems they have to deal with. One of these in particular is that due to the imperfections in the aggregate, concrete can fail in unexpected ways.

Further to this I worked at Bespak, a company manufacturing complex medical devices, including respirators and dose counters. One of the main reasons I decided on engineering was this experience. I was given two assignments to improve their current products; one to find an alternative mechanism to allow a tracheotomy device to work in a MRI scanner and the other to design the mechanism for a pocket dose counter. Although I did not find a definitive solution to these problems, I produced designs and ideas that were put into use including a plastic spring for the tracheotomy device, something the company had not thought of before. I really enjoyed the entire experience; particularly being part of a problem-solving team. I also did some work experience with Palm Paper, which has recently set up the largest paper processing plant in Europe outside King's Lynn, which was fascinating, seeing this huge plant being set up, and manufacturing on such an enormous scale.

To further my knowledge of science and engineering I am now subscribing to *New Scientist* and also I am going to lectures at the Royal Society. One of my great loves is ancient history and as an engineer I was stunned by the achievements of the ancient Greeks on a recent tour of the ancient sites. Having read *Structures* by J.E. Gordon, I began to really appreciate how impressive some of these sites were.

I enjoy classical music and play the double bass with the school orchestra. It is a really rewarding experience when the whole piece comes together and a great team exercise as it relies on everyone to play their part right. I also have recently been stage manager for a school play which required a lot of organisation and leadership to make sure everyone was in the right place at the right time with their particular props. I have greatly enjoyed playing rugby for a school team for which I was made captain and running the local 10k marathon, which I have done three times in aid of the local hospice. Lastly, I am an avid reader, enjoying a complete cross-section of styles and subjects.

Personal statement 2

Character count (with spaces): 3,715

I have admired the power of science ever since my physics teacher taught me the theories and laws of physics. Why does Newton's law of gravitation work? How come energy is always conserved? And most importantly, how can these rules benefit us? AS chemistry has sparked my interest in environmental issues, such as the effect of chlorofluorocarbons on the depletion of the ozone layer and what the connection between bond polarity and climate change could be. Core maths, in turn, has proved to me that mathematics is a very useful tool in modelling the environment: it taught me that exponential growth and decay graphs can be used to predict the population of an animal species, such as elephants. Throughout AS physics I have learnt important skills in experimental technique and analysis of data which are essential in engineering.

Yet nothing focused my interest in the subject as much as my recent work experience at Agip KCO's permitting and regulatory compliance department. Here I took my interest to a different level. I learnt about the process of environmental impact assessment and was astonished by how long this process takes, from the examination of the environmental condition before the exploration of oil and gas can begin to the risk assessment of offshore works. What particularly interested me was the attention to detail given when analysing the habitat of the flora and fauna of the Caspian Sea, ranging from little plankton to the population of seagulls. I was so excited by the intense focus of their work, that I continued reading outside school. I particularly enjoyed reading J.E. Gordon's 'New Science of Strong Materials'. It has increased my interest in engineering as it helped me to understand the essential link between the physical properties of materials, brittle and ductile, weak and strong, and how this is related to their chemical structures and bonds. Crystals can be both brittle but hard and be used in the production of high strength materials in the chemical industry. I was astounded to find out that a material can grow its own whiskers! I decided then that I wanted to pursue engineering as a career.

Indeed, I have taken every opportunity to learn about engineering and its impact on a global level. In 2008 I attended the Global Young Leaders Conference in the USA where I took part in the Model UN, representing India. GYLC has introduced me to the importance of international relations when proposing a common resolution to environmental problems such as global warming. I realised the significant connection between geopolitical issues and environmental engineering during the debates I took part in. These kinds of activities have demonstrated to me the importance of team work.

GYLC then led on to my being invited to the Presidential Youth Inaugural Conference for Barack Obama and receiving the Certificate of Ecological Hope for active participation in the scope of sustainable development from the Ministry of Environmental Protection of Kazakhstan. I have also been involved in a wide range of school events, such as the high school graduate ceremony as the narrator of the show and as a performer in an Italian dance team on intercultural awareness day. I have been playing the piano for more than eight years and have often performed Kazakh compositions on national holidays at school celebrations.

My belief is that there is still much more to explore and many questions to ask in the world of science and I am very excited to embark on a degree in engineering and ready to take up the challenge it poses. I am looking forward to solving environmental issues, and perhaps, sometime in the future, I will carry out my own environmental impact assessment.

Personal statement 3

Character count (with spaces): 3,863

I believe the modern world would be nothing without the breakthroughs engineers and scientists have made. I want to be a part of this process. I always pulled radios and watches apart, but it was aeroplanes that first drew me to science. I remember sitting by the window, grinning as the wing flaps flexed, while other passengers gripped the armrests, and whispered prayers. I couldn't understand how anyone was afraid of flight. I am intrigued by how devices work, from simple electric motors to the principles of winglets on aeroplane wings, and by machines and systems especially those that are theoretical or even fantastical.

I became interested in physics outside the classroom a couple of years ago. I've spent a lot of time reading ('New Scientist' and various websites) about mechanical processes, such as internal combustion, motorbikes' counter-steering, water saws, artificial gravity in space, and astroengineering, especially LaGrange points and space elevators. I am following the efforts of the Japan Space Elevator Association to begin design and production. I find the progress being made in the field of Nuclear Fusion inspiring, especially after seeing a documentary on the development of HiPER. The use of lasers and mirrors was revelatory: the idea that a power station could create MeV of energy from isotopes in sea water seemed like science fiction but wasn't. I plan to visit the construction site of ITER next year to explore the practical side of nuclear physics and see how the theory I've learnt is applied in the real world. I heard a great Design London talk at Imperial College by Dick Powell about the connections between creative thinking, design and real world applications. Part of my desire to be an engineer comes from the solutions that science can provide – clean and sustainable energy, for example especially in light of the BP crisis in the Gulf of Mexico; or safety and recovery issues highlighted by the stunning rescue of the Chilean miners. There is such a range of exciting projects; from the LHC at CERN, which I visited on a school trip, where I first began to understand that, while in theory nuclear physics happened on a small scale, the real world applications were massive; to the inventiveness of the 'barefoot engineers', like William Kamkwamba who built a wind-powered generator, using bicycle parts, plastic pipes and simple motors.

My interest in RE and ancient cultures (the ethics and philosophy behind science) has broadened my interest in engineering by adding a sociological element. I have been lucky enough to travel widely, and seen several impressive engineering achievements; the Sydney Opera House and the Harbour Bridge are two I will never forget. Jorn Utzon's ingenious interlocking shells showed me how design and practical engineering are so interdependent – a life-altering moment. Recently travelling in Israel and witnessing the huge Jewish settlements erected in months rather than years was amazing. Trekking to the ancient city of Petra in Jordan, carved out of mountains, made me understand that even 2,000 years ago the principles of engineering and design were just as vital and universal then as now.

I was an intern at the design company Publicreative, indexing, using Photoshop and developing my people skills. In this gap year I have planned work experience for WSP Group, as well as at Meggitt's and Classic Aero Engineering, restoring a Spitfire and a Hurricane.

Music is another passion: playing saxophone in the school jazz band for 10 years meant lots of concerts at school, the Eisteddford, in London and Paris. I am a good listener and team player. I enjoyed volunteering at a local primary school and helping children to read.

I am fascinated by the principles and practice of engineering and look forward to the challenge and excitement that university life will bring.

Personal statement 4

Character count (with spaces): 3,454

Engineering plays a role in everything we do in society, from building infrastructure to making our lives easier, for example through electronics. I hope that in my future as an engineer I will have the chance to play a role in making an impact on the way we move forward in these challenging times.

I have always been intrigued by mathematics and I chose to take the mechanics options due to my love of physics and the application of maths to our environment, for example in the creation of new bridges. Physics has given me a foundation for engineering and it has also enabled me to improve on my practical skills and my ability to minimise errors, a skill which I have appreciated during my A level course. Books such as 'The New Science of Strong Materials: Or Why Things Don't Fall Through the Floor' by J.E. Gordon and programmes about engineering feats are very thought provoking and educational. Attending lectures and day courses at Imperial College London and at UCL increased my interest in science and engineering as they broadened my knowledge of maths and physics and their usefulness to the structures we see around us, such as studying the way different forces interact on an object.

I have volunteered at the Royal Institution during their family fun days for the last two years and I am an assistant teacher for the mathematics master classes for year nines also run by the RI, both of which have allowed me to work as a team member with new people and look at science and mathematics from a variety of different academic levels. Communicating ideas is a very useful skill to any engineer as it is always necessary to be able to work as a team and ensure each person's role comes together. I have been debating since Year Nine, during which time I have entered the Rotary Club Debating competition and participated in school debating competitions, all of which have improved my team working skills and also my confidence as a public speaker, especially when marketing ideas. As a senior prefect at both my previous schools, I have been able to experience a sense of greater responsibility towards others that has enhanced my ability to collaborate with people. I was also editor of the Sacred Heart High School newsletter, where I managed to raise enough money to expand the scale and scope of the paper.

Being able to communicate in Spanish is a useful skill which I will be using to do a four-week placement at the department of toxicology at the University of Seville, where I will be studying and researching about the contamination of the sea by cities' residual waters. Working in Spanish will be a very useful skill to me as an engineer as it will allow me to communicate and work with people abroad. Additionally, I have organised placements with engineering companies, such as Amec and Arup, in order to gain more work experience over next Easter and summer. I have participated in three French exchanges during the last four years which have allowed me to maintain a basic level of French, a skill I hope to improve at university.

I am interested in studying civil engineering as I would like my role as an engineer to have a positive effect on altering our lives, while sustaining our environment. This is the reason that I have chosen the course which allows me to learn not only civil engineering but also link it in with the environment. I am excited to start this new phase of my life and look forward to learning new skills.

Work experience

Work experience is important as it demonstrates a commitment to the subject outside the classroom. Remember to include any experience, paid or voluntary. If you have had relevant work experience, mention it on your form. Explain concisely what your job entailed and what you got out of the whole experience. Even if you have not been able to get work experience, if you have spoken to anyone in engineering about their job it is worth mentioning as all this information builds up a picture of some-one who is keen and has done some research. See Chapter 3 for further information.

General tips

- Keep a copy of your personal statement so you can remind yourself of all the wonderful things you said about yourself, should you be called for interview!
- Print off a copy of your application to remind yourself what you have said. Before submitting it, also ensure you check your application through very carefully for careless errors which are harder to see on screen.
- Ensure that you have actually done all the things you mentioned in the statement by the time you are interviewed.

Summary

The seven steps to writing a successful personal statement are as follows.

1. Research the course content.
2. Research the entry requirements.
3. Find out your grade predictions.
4. Ensure your personal statement is directed at the courses you are applying for.
5. Include sufficient detail in the personal statement.
6. Illustrate your points with examples and evidence.
7. Remember every word in a personal statement counts.

3 | Work experience and the gap year

Work experience

Work experience is an invaluable way of demonstrating to the universities that you are committed to the course you are applying for. Work experience will also show you whether you are suitable for a career in engineering, and what qualities are needed in a successful engineer. One of the things that an admissions tutor will look for is how serious you are about your chosen course. Work experience or work-shadowing is an ideal way to demonstrate your commitment and show that you have done some research. If you can write about things that you saw or did on your work placement, and how they related to your A level studies, proposed university course, or future career, you will become a much more attractive proposition to the university selectors.

Recent surveys have highlighted the importance that engineering employers attach to internships and work experience. And this is also true of your university application. As more and more students chase a fixed number of places, preference is given to those candidates who can demonstrate that they have made an effort to find out what working within the field of engineering will be like.

What will you gain from work experience?

- It will add weight to your personal statement.
- It will give you a true insight into engineering and whether or not that is what you want to do. Some real experience will be particularly useful if you are trying to weigh up which area of engineering you would like to go into. For example, are you more practically or theoretically minded? Would you be more suited to a career in mechanical engineering or electronic engineering?
- It gives you the opportunity to build up those all-important contacts.
- It will add weight to your curriculum vitae (CV) – and will help you to gain references, which are important for any future career.

Looking for work experience

Marketing yourself

Some schools will arrange work experience for their (fortunate) students, but most people have to arrange it for themselves.

So how do you get work experience?

- You could approach local companies, or use any contacts that your family may have.
- The institutes of engineering have contacts with engineering companies so try to go through them (see contact details in Chapter 9).
- There are many schemes operated by universities and the engineering institutes aimed at attracting students into engineering, and these often involve work placements.

If you have a contact in a local engineering firm, try asking to go in for one or two weeks' work experience or work-shadowing during the holidays. Remember that even a single day of work-shadowing is better than no evidence of experience within the workplace. Whichever route you take, it will almost certainly be on a voluntary basis unless. If that is the case, you could try to get some paid work during the summer or register with an employment agency.

How to apply for work experience

The first thing you need to do is to put together a CV. This is a summary of what you have done in your life to date. If you have hardly any previous work experience, then one page on good quality A4 paper will be sufficient. If you are a mature student with a lot of jobs behind you, there is sometimes a case for going on to a second page, but for most young people a brief CV will be appropriate.

Here is the information that you will need to include:

- full name
- address, telephone number and e-mail address
- date of birth
- nationality
- education – places, qualifications and grades (start with the most recent)
- skills (e.g. computer skills, software packages you are familiar with, languages spoken, whether you hold a driving licence)
- work experience (full time or part time, with names and addresses of the companies or businesses and a brief description of your responsibilities)

- positions of responsibility
- hobbies
- names and contact details of two or three people who can act as your referees.

Always draw attention to your good points on your CV that will highlight your interest in engineering. Do not leave gaps, that is, always account for your time. If something such as illness prevented you from reaching your potential in your exams, point this out in your covering letter. Remember, both your CV and covering letter need to have perfect spelling and grammar in order to be looked at and considered seriously so take the time to check them thoroughly.

A sample CV

Lay out your CV clearly and logically, avoiding gaps, and including any exams you are studying for as well as those taken. Below is an example.

Jonathan Luke

Address: 1 Heggie Road, Edinburgh EH2 3EF

Telephone: 0123 456 7890
Email: jl@whizzmail.co.uk

Date of birth: 1 January 1992
Nationality: British

Education 2003–10: Edinburgh High School
2010: A levels to be taken: Physics, Chemistry, Mathematics
2009: AS level: Geography (B)
2008: GCSEs: English (A), Mathematics (A), Geography (A), German (A), Biology (B), Chemistry (B), History (C), Physics (C)

Work experience
2008–10 (Saturdays)
Sales Assistant in Heggie's Department Store.
Responsible for operating the checkouts during busy times; dealing with customer enquiries and complaints; checking till receipts against takings.
The job requires good communication skills, the ability to deal sympathetically with complaints, and accuracy in dealing with the financial aspects of the post.

Skills
Modern languages: good written and spoken German.
IT: competent in MS Word, PowerPoint and Excel, good keyboard skills.

Positions of responsibility
Captain of school volleyball team, treasurer for the school film society.

Interests
Volleyball, swimming, reading, film, travel and music.

References
Available on request.

The covering letter

Every CV or application form should always be accompanied by a covering letter. The letter is important because it is usually the first thing a potential employer reads. Here are some tips on structuring and presenting your letter.

- Use good quality unlined A4 paper.
- Try to find out the name of the person to whom you should send your letter and CV. It makes a great difference to the reader the more you can personalise your application, but make sure that you adhere to the conventions of style with regard to business letters. Get a book on business letter writing if you need help. For instance, if you start the letter 'Dear Mr Brown' remember you should finish it 'Yours sincerely'. If you do not know the recipient's name and send it, for example, to the personnel manager, you should begin with 'Dear Sir or Madam' and finish with 'Yours faithfully'.
- The first paragraph should tell the recipient why you are contacting them (for example 'I am writing to enquire whether you have any openings for work experience').
- The second paragraph should give them some information to make them interested in you by highlighting your interest in engineering along with some specific skills you can offer, such as knowledge of word processing or having a good telephone manner.
- The letter should address the reasons why you want to work for that company. This should highlight your interest in what the company does and how this has a direct bearing on your own interest in the field of engineering.

- Use a word processor unless the company specifically requests a handwritten one.

Whether you are applying for a position through an advertisement or just sending a speculative letter to a local company, you should do plenty of research on the employer. Having some information will help you tailor your CV for that particular company, and it will certainly be impressive if at interview you show some knowledge of how the company works.

If you have an application form to fill in, follow the instructions carefully. Always complete forms neatly, using black ink. If your handwriting can be unclear, make sure that you take your time. You probably will not be asked to submit your CV as well, so always add evidence to support the statements in your application forms.

It is imperative that you keep copies of all the letters, CVs and application forms you send off, not just so you can remember to whom you have applied, but so that you have something to work from at an interview. You are bound to be asked to elaborate on things you have written about yourself, so do not say you have got a skill or an interest if you cannot back it up.

Work experience interviews

Most of the tips mentioned in the next chapter would equally apply if you are going for an interview for work experience. Some additional tips are given below.

- Think through why you want the job, and in particular why you want to work for that organisation.
- Research the employer thoroughly before interview. Look at their brochure and website.
- Plan in advance what you think your key selling points are to the employer and make sure you find an opportunity in the interview to get these across.
- Prepare a few questions to ask your interviewer at the end. You can demonstrate your preparation here by asking them about something you have read about the company recently, if appropriate.
- Remember to shake hands in a nice, firm, and confident way at the beginning and end of the interview.

Taking a gap year

Many students take a gap year between their final school or college examinations and the start of their university course. Universities are nearly always happy with this as students who take a year away from studies are often more motivated and mature when they start their degree studies. But in terms of the application, a gap year will only enhance your chances of getting a place if you use the year productively.

There are two application routes for students taking a gap year:

- You can apply for deferred entry, that is, applying in the final year of the A level course for entry a year later. So, if you are sitting A levels in June 2011 you would apply for entry in September/October 2012, not 2011.
- Alternatively, you can apply at the start of the gap year, once your A level results are known.

There are advantages to both routes, depending on your plans and A level grades.

Advantages of deferred entry

- You will know where you are going to study in August, before you start your gap year, and so you can focus your thoughts and energies on your gap year projects.
- You will not need to interrupt your gap year plans for interviews, which may be difficult to do if you are planning to spend some months abroad.
- If you are unsuccessful in getting offers from your chosen universities or courses, you can reapply during the gap year.

Advantages of applying during the gap year

- You have more time to decide which field of engineering really interests you.
- You will know your examination grades and so you can target your application much more effectively.
- If your predicted grades are not high enough, but you feel confident in achieving better than the predictions, you do not run the risk of being rejected based on the predictions.

Whichever route you take, you must plan the gap year properly so that it is clear to the universities that you (and they) will benefit from it. The point of the gap year is to gain experience, maturity, and independence, or to earn money to help to fund your studies. A year spent sleeping and watching television, however attractive that may be after all the hard work you put into your school examinations, is not going to convince the universities that you will be a stronger candidate as a result.

Here is an excerpt from a personal statement:

> *'I am taking a gap year in order to gain more maturity and experience.'*

Such a statement is not going to convince the admissions tutors that you have made constructive plans for your gap year, nor is it likely to help you develop or bring new skills and ideas onto their courses.

A better statement might be:

> *'During my gap year, I have arranged a placement with a local company that manufactures electric motors. This will be useful because it will give me an insight into the whole process of commercial production as well as giving me a chance to learn more about the practical uses of mechanical and electrical engineering. As an engineer, you have to be aware of issues such as cost-effectiveness, safety, and environmental issues as well as the technical side. I will also work part time in a local petrol station to earn some money for my travels. This will help me to improve my communication skills. In February I have planned a trip to Thailand, Vietnam, and Cambodia. I will then go to Australia for two months to work with my uncle who is an architect, and I hope to learn more about the process of turning designs into real buildings.'*

This is much more impressive because the candidate has linked what she will do in her gap year to her future degree course (electrical engineering), and it is clear that she has thought carefully about what she will do during the year.

A piece of advice: phrases such as 'I have arranged to . . .' are much more convincing than 'I hope to . . .' when discussing your gap year plans.

Gap year plans

It is always a good idea to check with your chosen universities that a gap year is acceptable to them before committing yourself. There is likely to be information on their websites addressing this. If there is none, you can email the admissions staff to ask them. This is particularly important if you are taking a gap year for reasons other than wanting to take a year between school studies and the degree course to gain experience in engineering.

Some of the other reasons for taking a gap year are:

- to work towards extra qualifications because you need to strengthen your application, or because you wish to change direction (for example if you had studied mathematics up to AS level only, you will be doing an evening class in A2 mathematics alongside your other projects)
- you started another course (such as a degree course in another subject) and then realised that it is not right for you, so you have withdrawn from it
- you have been working, and you now want to return to studying
- you may have had an illness or other issues that required you to take a break from studying.

4 | Succeeding at interview

Although many universities do not interview prospective students, a number (including Imperial College, Oxford, and Cambridge) still do. If you are invited for an interview, here are some points to bear in mind.

- Your interview will decide whether you will be offered a place or not. The information on the UCAS application will have been the basis on which the decision to interview you was made, but a good UCAS form cannot help after a poor interview. So prepare thoroughly.
- If you interview well, and you subsequently narrowly miss the grades that you need to take the place, you may still be offered the place.
- Interviews need not be as daunting as you fear. Interviews are designed to help those asking the questions to find out as much about you as they can. It is important to make eye contact and show confident body language – and treat the experience positively as a chance to put yourself across well rather than as an obstacle course designed to catch you out.
- Go into the interview with a mental checklist of what points you wish to mention in the interview and try to steer the interview to address these (see below).
- Interviewers are less interested in investigating your subject knowledge than in looking at how suitable and committed you are for their course. So, evidence of research and appropriate qualities such as analytical or problem-solving skills are important elements of a successful interview.
- Remember your future tutor might be among the people interviewing you. Enthusiasm and a strong commitment to your subject and above all, willingness to learn, are extremely important attitudes to convey.
- An ability to think on your feet is vital – another prerequisite for a career in engineering. Pre-learned answers never work. Putting forward an answer using examples and factual knowledge to reinforce your points will impress interviewers far more. Essential preparation includes revision of the personal statement section of your UCAS application; so never include anything in your UCAS application that you are not prepared to speak about at an interview.
- Questions may well be asked on your extracurricular activities. This is often a tactic designed to put you at your ease and to find out about the sort of person you are; therefore your answers should be thorough and enthusiastic.

- At the end of the interview, you will probably be asked if there is anything you would like to ask your interviewer. If there is nothing you wish to ask, do say that your interview has covered all that you had thought of. It is sensible, though, to have one or two questions of a serious kind up your sleeve – to do with the course, the tuition, and so on. But it is not wise to ask anything that you could and should have found out from the prospectus.
- Above all, end on a positive note and remember to smile! Make them remember you when they go through a list of 20 or more candidates at the end of the day.

Advice from an admissions tutor

'Within the Department of EEE, we actively encourage all applicants that are expected to meet our very high entry standards to attend their interview afternoon. The reason is not to test their academic ability, but to ensure that they have what it takes to succeed at Imperial in their studies. Perhaps more importantly, we want our high-calibre students to be happy during their stay at Imperial and so it is important to know that they want to study EEE for the right reasons. To this end, during their interview, we are looking for a student that is 'switched on' (as opposed to an applicant having been primed for the occasion) and genuinely keen to pursue a career in EEE (it is not uncommon for parents to push their children into this subject). We ask each applicant a few technical questions, of increasing difficulty, to gauge their limits of mathematics and physics; not necessarily related to EEE. In addition, we are looking for a confident inquisitive mind, as well as signs of weakness areas. Since places are limited, we try to find signs that the applicant will have a long-term commitment to academic life, as well as indicators that suggest that they will help to enrich the lives of those around them.'

Dr Stepan Lucyszyn, Undergraduate Admissions Tutor for the Department of Electrical and Electronic Engineering (EEE) at Imperial College London

Steering the interview

There will be issues that you want to raise in the interview, things that will demonstrate your research, commitment, and personal qualities. Rather than walk out of the interview disappointed that you did not have the opportunity to discuss these things, try to bring them into the conversation. For example, you may have been to a lecture on developments within the electronics industry at a local university one evening and you want to talk about this. There are likely to be many ways that you can do this. You might be asked why you want to be an engineer, and during your answer you could say 'and the thing that really convinced me that electronic engineering was the right career for me was listening to Professor Smith talking about nanotechnology at a lecture that I attended at Surrey University last month.'

In all probability, the interviewer will then ask you more about this, and you can then talk about something that you know about, rather than having to face questions on a topic with which you are less familiar.

Before you go to the interview, write down a list of things you want to talk about, and think of ways that you may be able to do so.

Preparing for an interview

Preparation for an interview should be an intensification of the work you are already doing outside class for your A level courses. Interviewers will be looking for evidence of an academic interest and commitment that extends beyond the classroom. They will also be looking for an ability to apply the theories and methods that you have been learning in your A level courses to the real world.

Essentially, the interview is a chance for you to demonstrate knowledge of, commitment to, and enthusiasm for engineering. The only way to do this is by trying to be as well informed as you can. Interviewers will want to know your reasons for wishing to study engineering and the best way to demonstrate this is with examples of things you have seen, read about, or researched.

Newspapers and magazines

Before your interview it is vital that you are aware of current affairs related to the course for which you are being interviewed. The *New Scientist* will give you a good grasp of scientific and engineering developments, as will reading the science sections of the broadsheet newspapers. You should also keep up to date with current affairs in general.

Magazines can be an important source of comment on current issues and deeper analysis. There are many specialist engineering publications, such as *The Engineer*, *New Civil Engineer*, and *Aviation Week*. Further details can be found in Chapter 9.

Television and radio

It is also important to watch or listen to the news every day, again paying particular attention to news about scientific and engineering issues. Documentaries and programmes about engineering projects can be enormously helpful in showing how what you are studying is applied to actual situations and events. Keep an eye on the television schedules for programmes or series on anything related to your field of interest, which could range from those aimed at a wide audience (*Grand Designs*, *James May's Big Ideas*, and *Richard Hammond's Engineering Connections*) to more factual programmes such as *Horizon*. BBC Radio 4's series *Frontiers* and *Material World* are also very useful.

The internet

A wealth of easily accessible, continually updated and useful information is, it goes without saying, available on the internet. Given the ease with which information can be accessed, there is really no excuse for not being able to keep up to date with relevant current issues. Radio programmes can be downloaded as podcasts and listened to at times convenient to you; the BBC's iPlayer gives access to current affairs and documentary programmes for up to a week after they have been broadcast; iTunesU gives free access to thousands of lectures and presentations from universities around the world; newspapers can be read online . . . the list is endless. In this age of information overload, anyone who is serious about keeping abreast of current issues (or wants to be seen as being serious) has unlimited opportunities to do so. Thus, an interviewer is not going to be impressed with a student who claims he/she has been too busy to know what is happening in his/her chosen areas of interest.

- Subscribe to podcasts and download them regularly. BBC podcasts, which are free, include *Frontiers* and *Material World*.
- Check online news websites every day to read the latest news stories.
- If you cannot buy a newspaper every day, look at an online version, for example www.guardian.co.uk.

Examples of your areas of interest

One way to make an interview a success is to illustrate the points you are making with examples. It is also easier to talk about something you know about rather than trying to talk in general terms. And if the examples you use are interesting, the interviewer may well want to talk about them rather than ask you the next question on his/her list. But remember, this will only work if you have done your research beforehand. There is nothing worse in an interview than a conversation along the lines of:

You: One of the things that inspired me study civil engineering was a journey with my parents up the east coast of England, when we crossed the Humber Bridge, the first suspension bridge I had ever seen at first hand.

Interviewer: I see. Can you tell me something about the reasons for building a suspension bridge there rather than a more traditional bridge?
You: Sorry, I don't know.

A better answer would have been:

You: The Humber estuary is used for shipping, and because of the width of the estuary, a traditional beam or cantilever structure would not have been able to span the space between the banks. Also, suspension bridges have some flexibility and that area is prone to high winds.

The interviewer might then have gone on to discuss the types of forces that are present in a suspension bridge, and about suitable materials, all of which you would be familiar with because you had anticipated this response and had prepared for it.

Here are some ideas to use as examples to illustrate points you want to make:

- names and construction details of a few buildings, bridges, etc.
- examples of machines that you can discuss (cars, aircraft, wind turbines, etc.)
- an industrial chemical process
- a medical breakthrough that was developed by engineers (such as computerised tomography (CT) scanners)
- the background on the development of, for example, solid state memory for computers
- developments in energy sources such as fuel cells or hybrid motors
- the changing face of computing – from mainframe computers to smartphones.

The interview

Interview questions are likely to test your knowledge of engineering projects and developments in the real world since, unlike some theoretical science subjects, engineering is a practical subject aimed at making the world a better place. It is important that your answers are delivered in appropriate language. You will impress interviewers with fluent use of precise technical terms, and thus detailed knowledge of the definitions of words and phrases used in engineering is essential. Potential electrical engineers need to know the technical and microscopic differences between semiconductors and insulators, and to be able to differentiate clearly between electric charge and current; and if you are interested in materials or civil engineering, you need to use words such as *stress, strain, elasticity, strength, toughness,* and *stiffness* with their scientific, rather than everyday, meanings.

You might be asked which part of your A level courses you have most enjoyed. You need to think carefully about this before interview and, if possible, steer the interview in the direction of these topics so that you can display your knowledge.

Future plans and possible careers may also be discussed at interview. You will not be expected to have completely made up your mind about this but, by the same token, you will not be held to what you say at interview after you have left university. Previous work experience is useful and you should be able to recall the precise tasks you carried out during your employment and think about them before interview so that you can answer questions on them fully and well. Questions of this kind will be asked to see if you have an understanding of how business and management theories and methods are actually applied in the world outside school or college.

Interviewers will ask questions with a view to being in a position to form an opinion about the quality of your thought and your ability to negotiate. You may be presented with a real or supposed set of circumstances and then be asked to comment on their business implications.

Do not forget that interview skills are greatly improved by practice. Talk through the issues we have discussed with your friends and then request a careers officer, teacher, or family friend to give you a mock interview.

In any interview situation it makes a better impression if you arrive in plenty of time for your interview and dress smartly and appropriately (people in business tend to look quite formal). Try to appear confident and enthusiastic in your interview – but listen carefully to the questions you are asked without interrupting and always answer honestly.

50 sample interview questions

1. What first started your interest in engineering?
2. Why do you want to be an engineer?
3. What qualities does it take to be a successful engineer?
4. What have you done to investigate engineering as a course?
5. What have you done to investigate engineering as a career?
6. What field of engineering particularly interests you?
7. What is the difference between science and engineering?
8. What is the difference between science and technology?
9. Give me a very brief outline of the key engineering developments of the 20th/21st century.
10. What do you consider to be the most significant engineering project in history?
11. Do you have an engineering hero/heroine?
12. What did you learn from your work experience at X Enterprises?

13. How does the structure of a metal determine its properties?

14. Why does the molecular structure of wood make it suitable for some building projects but not others?

15. What is the difference between a 'tough' material and a 'strong' material?

16. What do we mean by potential difference?

17. What is the difference between charge and current?

18. How did the invention of the silicon chip revolutionise communication?

19. How does the internet work?

20. What is a robot?

21. In what situation do you think the distinction between artificial and human intelligence become indistinguishable?

22. Why are the concrete girders used to construct buildings 'T' shaped in cross-section?

23. Can you explain what is meant by 'proof by induction'?

24. Can a scientific theory ever be proved?

25. What is meant by conservation of energy?

26. Murphy's law says that whatever can go wrong will go wrong, for example if you drop a piece of bread that has jam on one side on the floor, it will always fall with the jam side down. How would you go about verifying Murphy's law?

27. Which parts of the electromagnetic spectrum can humans detect?

28. What is a machine?

29. What is a computer?

30. What is a bit and what is a byte?

31. What is 27 in binary? What would it be in a system based on the number 4 rather than 2? Or in a number system based on the number 9?

32. Why is nano-technology so called?

33. How does a car engine work?

34. Why is distance that an electric vehicle can travel so small compared with a petrol-fuelled vehicle?

35. What is a semi-conductor?

36. How does an aircraft stay in the air when it is more dense than air?

37. What is meant by the words 'digital' and 'analogue' when describing communication systems such as TV signals?

38. People describe new inventions as being the most significant since 'the invention of the wheel'. How do you think the wheel was invented?

39. People describe a good idea as being 'the best thing since sliced bread' – what are the advantages and disadvantages of sliced bread?

40. Why does a bicycle have gears?
41. How does the car braking system work?
42. What limits the maximum height of a proposed new office development?
43. What is meant by a 'cantilever'? How do the stresses on a bridge using cantilevers differ from a bridge using a beam to span the distance between two supports?
44. An architect designs a new 50 storey office building. How might an engineer test whether it is safe to build it?
45. An architect designs a steel and glass bridge. How might an engineer test whether it is safe to build it?
46. A designer creates a model for a new type of passenger aircraft. How might an engineer test whether it is safe to build it?
47. What is bio-technology?
48. What is the Born–Haber process?
49. The first world war was described as being the 'chemists' war', and the second world war the 'physicists' war'. Why is this?
50. Describe this (*showing the student an everyday object – a chair, a frying pan, a light bulb, a shoe, a watch*) from an engineering perspective.

How to answer interview questions

Introductory questions

Why have you chosen to apply here?

The interviewer will need to be reassured that you have done your research, and that you are applying to the university for the right reasons, rather than because your friend tells you that the social life at that particular university is excellent. Your answer should, if possible, include the following points:

- first-hand knowledge of the university, for example you came to an open day, or you have spoken to students who have studied there. If you cannot visit the university, then at least try to discuss the institution with current or ex-students. Many university websites have links to current students who can answer your questions directly
- detailed knowledge of the course and why it is attractive to you, or how it links to your future career plans. The course might, for example, offer the chance to learn a language as one of the options in Year 2, and you could mention this as being something that will help you to work overseas. Or it might offer work placements or the chance to spend a period of time at an overseas university.

Why do you want to be an engineer?

(This question, or a variant on it – What have you done to investigate engineering? When did you decide that engineering was the right course for you? – will almost certainly be asked. It would be considered by the interviewers to be a gentle introduction to the interview because they will assume that you have thought about this, and anticipated it being asked.)

Your answer should include an indication of how your interest started (for example taking apart a radio, building a model out of Lego, something you were taught in a science lesson) and lead on to things you have done to investigate engineering. This would, ideally, involve work experience or an engineering lecture you went to. You could end up by talking about a particular area of interest (mechanical engineering, civil engineering) or a project that interests you (a building, a machine?) and possible plans for your future career.

General questions about engineering

What qualities should an engineer possess?

(Variants on this question might include 'From your work experience, what did you learn about what it takes to be a successful engineer?')

Points you might raise could include: mathematical ability, logic, analytical and problem-solving skills, curiosity. But it is important to expand on these rather than simply list them. Explain, ideally using an example to illustrate what you are saying, why you think that this quality is important. Examples can be drawn from your work experience, your wider reading, or a lecture.

Here is an example:

> 'The ability to solve problems is very important. I really became aware of this when I was doing my work experience at a local engineering company. They were making low voltage lamps for use in recessed lighting fittings in houses and offices, but in one particular building, the lamps kept blowing. In the end, one of the engineers decided that the problem must have been in the transformer rather than the lamp itself, and so he looked at where the transformers for each lamp were situated. It turned out that they were short-circuiting because the cavity above the false ceiling was damp.'

What does a mechanical engineer do?

(Variants on this could include asking for definitions of engineering, science, or technology.)

Again, try to illustrate your answer with an example or the details of a conversation that you had with an engineer: 'Mechanical engineers work with machines. But I know from the work experience that I did at my local garage that understanding about the mechanical aspects of, for example, a car engine is only a small part of it. You need to have a good knowledge of electricity and confidence with computers, since a lot of the trouble-shooting was done using electronic equipment.'

Questions designed to assess your clarity of thought

You may be given an open-ended question about something you have already studied. The point of this type of question is not so much to test your knowledge or academic level (because this will be clear in the grade predictions and exam results on the UCAS application) but to see if you can think logically and in a structured way. So, your answer should really be an exercise in 'thinking aloud', that is, talking the interviewer through the steps to your final answer. An example is given below.

Why are metals so useful to engineers?

You could start from first principles by describing the microscopic struc-ture of a metal. This shows that you can approach problems in a logical way while also giving you some time to think about where your answer is going: 'A metallic structure consists of a lattice of positive ions sur-rounded by a "sea" of delocalised electrons. It is this structure that gives metals their useful properties.'

You might then go on to look at a number of properties in detail: 'The most obvious properties this gives metals are good electrical and ther-mal conductivity. Electrical conduction is through the flow of electrons through the lattice, and since they are not attached to any particular atom, they can move freely. Metals are also good conductors of heat because the electrons are able to transfer energy as they move in addi-tion to the vibrations of the lattice.'

You could then move on to other properties that make metals so useful, describing each one in turn. You would probably include malleability, and the use of physical processes to alter the strength, stiffness, or tough-ness of a metal to suit its intended usage.

Questions that assess your ability to analyse or to solve problems

You may well be confronted by a question about a situation that you have not covered in your studies. Don't worry. The interviewer will know that this is a new area for you. What he or she is looking for is not for you to immediately give them the correct answer, but rather, how you can take things that you know and apply them to new situations.

In 2009, applicants for one university were asked 'What percentage of the world's water is in one cow?' Of course, no one (including the person who asked the question) knows the answer to this. What they were interested in, as discussed in the previous example, was in the candidate's ability to approach a problem from first principles and to arrive at an answer in a logical and structured way. So, an answer of 'I don't know' would not be very useful to your chances of being offered a place.

A better answer might start with: 'Well, I suppose I might begin with trying to estimate how much water there is on Earth. I know from my physics what the radius of the Earth is, and so I could work out its volume. I could then make an assumption about the average depth of the oceans and work out their volume . . .' Rather than listen in silence, it is likely that the interviewer will help you by giving you hints or guiding you. But they can only do this if you explain every step.

When I talk to students about what they worry about when they are preparing for their interviews, they always say, 'What if I cannot answer a question?' And here is what I say to them.

1. Interviewers are aware of the level you have studied to, and so will have a good idea of what you should know and may not know.
2. Therefore, it is likely that any 'new' topic that you are confronted with at the interview has been asked to see *how you think* rather than *what you know*.
3. Approach all questions from first principles, for example GCSE knowledge, and then build up your answer.
4. If your answer requires you to draw a sketch or do a calculation, ask if you can use a piece of paper or the whiteboard in the interview room.
5. Don't be afraid to ask for help, but do this by asking for comments on what you think is the right approach: 'I think I would start by looking at the forces on the body – is this right?

Questions to show your interest in engineering

Anyone can say that they are interested in engineering, but by applying to study engineering at university, you are embarking not just on a short period of study but on your future career as well. An interviewer (who is almost certainly an engineer him/herself) will want to be reassured that you are serious enough about the profession to keep up to date with developments and engineering issues. So, questions such as 'Tell me about an engineering issue that you have read recently' are designed to see if you keep abreast of current events. How do you ensure that you are prepared for such questions?

- Watch the television or listen to the radio news on a daily basis. In 2010, two of the biggest and long-running news stories were about engineering projects that were undertaken in response to accidents – the BP Gulf of Mexico oil spill and the rescue of the Chilean miners (see also Chapter 8).
- Read the quality newspapers as often as you can, and keep a scrapbook of engineering-related stories.
- Check websites for engineering stories. A good starting point is the BBC website (www.bbc.co.uk), which has a section on science and technology.
- Visit the news sections of the websites of the engineering institutions and professional bodies (see pp. 95–97 for website addresses).
- Talk to engineers.
- If you can, go to public lectures at universities. Details can be found on the university websites.
- Watch podcasts of university lectures on iTunesU.
- Download or listen to radio programmes such as BBC Radio 4's *Material World*.

5 | Non-standard applications

This chapter applies to students who may be applying to university as mature students, perhaps with qualifications other than A levels or the equivalent, and to international students who are applying from outside the UK.

Perhaps you are studying for a mixture of examination qualifications, or you have had a gap in your education. You may have already started a degree course in another discipline and want to change direction. Whatever your situation, the first thing you should do is make contact with some universities (either by telephone or via the email addresses given on the university websites) to explain your situation and ask for advice.

We will look at two of the more common types of non-standard application in more detail: mature students and international students who are applying from their own countries. These candidates make up a small, but significant, proportion of those applying for engineering courses.

Mature students

Mature students fall into three categories:

1. those with appropriate qualifications, for example A levels, but who did not go to university and are now applying after a gap of a few years
2. those applying for a second degree, having graduated in a different discipline
3. those who have no A levels or equivalent qualifications.

If you are in the first two of these categories you can apply using the same route as first-time applicants. However, it is worth contacting universities directly to discuss your situation with them, and to get their advice.

Most universities encourage mature students to apply for entry to degree courses, taking into account their work experience and commitment as part of the entry criteria. Mature students have often:

- left school without the appropriate academic qualifications for university entrance in order to start jobs or careers
- studied at degree level in another, non-related, discipline.

There are many Access courses in colleges around the country that specifically prepare mature students for higher education. Universities often encourage mature students to apply because they:

- bring valuable real-life experience to the faculty
- can be more mature in their study methods than school-leavers
- have had more time to think about what they really want to study
- have a better understanding of the links between study and work.

The best way to find out about acceptable Access courses is to contact the universities directly and ask which ones they recognise or recommend. The engineering institutes (see Chapter 9 for a list of these) provide details of schemes that allow students who have studied on apprenticeship programmes to progress onto a higher national diploma or degree course.

If you are applying for a degree course as a mature student without using the Access course route, you should:

- use the UCAS 'Apply' system as described earlier in this book
- select 'no' to the question 'are you applying through your school or college' when prompted on the online application
- fill in the section on employment as comprehensively as possible, ensuring that there are no periods of time since you left school that are unaccounted for
- ask someone suitable (your current employer, a previous teacher) to act as your UCAS referee
- ensure that he/she knows what the universities require from the referee. You can point them towards the UCAS website, which has a section on information for referees.

International students

International students are usually:

- following A level (or equivalent) programmes either in the UK or in their home country
- studying for local qualifications that are recognised as being equivalent to A levels, in their own country
- studying on academic programmes that are not equivalent to A levels.

Students following A level or equivalent programmes should apply through UCAS in the usual way. All of the information in this book is equally applicable to them.

However, non-EU students will pay higher fees than UK or EU students. Whereas UK and EU students will pay around £3,500 a year for their degree courses (although this is likely to rise significantly as the UK government is currently reviewing the way universities are funded), students from outside these regions will pay in the region of £10,000–£20,000 a year for tuition. Accommodation and meals will be extra. How much living costs are depends on where you study, but as a rough guide, about £900 a month should cover food, accommodation, books, and some entertainment costs.

Students studying qualifications that are accepted in place of A levels can also apply through UCAS in the normal way, from their own country. The UCAS website (www.ucas.com) contains information on the equivalence of non-UK qualifications. These include the Irish Leaving Certificate, European Baccalaureate, and some international O levels and A levels. Information on the equivalence of other qualifications can be found on the UK government's qualifications website (www.naric.org.uk).

Students who do not have UK-recognised qualifications will need to follow a pre-university course before applying for the degree course. These include:

- university foundation courses at UK colleges and universities (these normally last one year)
- university foundation courses set up by, or approved by UK universities or colleges, but taught in the students' home countries
- A level courses (normally two years, but in some cases this can be condensed into one year) in schools and colleges in the UK. A levels allow students to apply to any of the UK universities, including the top-ranked universities such as Oxford, Cambridge, and Imperial College. Foundation courses are not recognised by all UK universities. You should check with your preferred universities about which courses they accept before committing yourself. Representatives of UK universities, schools and colleges regularly visit many countries around the world to promote their institutions and to give advice. You can also contact the British Council to get help with your application.

One of the reasons that international students are, on the face of it, less successful in their applications than UK students (see p. 31) is that they, their teachers, or their referees are unaware of what is required, particularly if they have experience of applications for universities in other countries. All of the information on personal statements and interviews in this book applies equally to UK and international students. If you are applying from outside the UK, you must ensure that your referee also understands what he/she needs to write. The UCAS website (www.ucas.com) contains a section giving advice to referees. In general, your referee should address the following points:

- some background information about you – a brief overview of your recent education, and why you are applying for a place at a UK university

- some background information about themselves – what their relationship is to you, how long they have known you, on what basis are they able to comment on your academic and personal qualities
- an assessment of your academic and personal strengths
- an assessment of your suitability for a course and career in engineering.

6 | What happens next

Replies from the universities

After your application has been assessed by the university, you will receive a response. You can also follow the progress of your application using the online Track facility on the UCAS website. You will receive one of three possible responses from each university:

- conditional offer
- unconditional offer
- rejection.

If you receive a conditional offer, you will be told what you need to achieve in your A levels. This could be in grade terms, for example AAB (and the university might specify a particular grade in a particular subject – AAB, with an A in mathematics), or in UCAS tariff points (300 points from three A levels – see Chapter 3). Unconditional offers can be given to students who have already sat their A levels, such as gap year students applying post-results. Rejection means that you have been unsuccessful in your application to that university.

Once you have received responses from all five universities, you will need to make your choice of the university offer you wish to accept. This is called your firm choice. You can also choose an insurance offer, effectively a second choice with a lower grade requirement. UCAS will give you a deadline of about a month from the date that you received your fifth response.

If you receive five rejections, then you can enter the UCAS Extra scheme, through which you can make additional choices.

Results day

- A levels – third week of August
- International Baccalaureate – early in July
- Scottish Highers – first week of August

Ask your school or college for the exact date and time that they will issue you with the results.

Whichever of the above 16+ exam systems you are sitting, you need to act quickly if you:

- have missed the grades or scores that you require to satisfy your firm offer
- are not holding any offers and wish to apply through Clearing (see p. 77)
- wish to use the Adjustment system (see p. 78).

What to do if things go wrong during the exams

Occasionally, students will underperform in an examination through no fault of their own. This could be through distressing family circumstances (a serious illness to a brother or sister, for example), illness in the run up to the exam (or during the exam) or unforeseen circumstances such as late arrival to the exam due to problems with public transport. In all cases, you should inform the universities that this has happened to you *immediately after the examination*. You should, if possible, get your referee to give the details to the universities and provide documentary evidence, such a letter from your general practitioner.

Table 1 gives a summary of your options.

Table 1 What you need to do after you get your 16+ results

Your results	Outcome	What you need to do
You have gained the grades that you need to satisfy your firm choice	You have your place	The university will contact you with confirmation of the place
You have gained grades that nearly meet those required for your firm choice (e.g. BBB for an ABB offer), but are good enough for your insurance offer	Your first choice can still accept you. Otherwise, you are automatically accepted onto the insurance place	Check on Track to see if you have been accepted. If not, contact the university and see if it can be persuaded to accept you. Your referee might be able to help with this
Your grades are well below those required for your firm choice, but satisfy your insurance offer	You are automatically accepted onto the insurance place	Check on Track to see if the insurance offer has been confirmed. If there seems to be a delay, contact the university
Your grades are below those needed for the insurance offer	You are now eligible for Clearing (see below)	Use the UCAS website and national newspapers to identify suitable courses from the published vacancies. Contact them by telephone

Your grades satisfy one of your offers, but you have changed your mind about the course you want to study	You can be considered for Clearing (see below) courses if you withdraw from your firm/insurance places	Contact UCAS to withdraw from your original place. Use the UCAS website and national newspapers to identify suitable courses from the published vacancies. Contact them by telephone
You have achieved grades that are not good enough to get you a Clearing place	You can be accepted onto Access, Diploma or Foundation places, and then progress on to a degree course. Alternatively, you can resit A levels and reapply next year	Discuss these options with your school and your parents. Don't make hasty decisions – ask the university to extend its deadline if necessary
You have done better than expected, and you have grades that match or exceed the standard offers for courses that you had not previously applied for; perhaps because you did not think that you would be considered by these universities because of your grade predictions	You have a short period of time to register for Adjustment (see below). This means that you hold on to your original offer but can also approach other universities to see if they have suitable vacancies that you could be considered for	Log onto 'Track' to register. Start telephoning universities
There are missing results (for example, an 'X' on your results slip rather than a grade	This probably means that there is an administrative error somewhere, for example, a missing coursework mark, or no 'cash-in' code for your AS and A2 exams	Contact your school or college examinations officer immediately to sort out the problem. Contact your firm and insurance choices and explain the situation to them and ask them to hold your place until the problem has been resolved

Clearing

Students who are not holding any offers when the examination results are published, or who have failed to achieve the grades that they need, can apply for vacancies through Clearing. The Clearing system operates by publishing all remaining university vacancies on the UCAS website and in the national newspapers. Students can then find appropriate courses and apply directly to the university. This time, you do not go through UCAS. UCAS will send you a Clearing Passport which, when you have been made a verbal offer that you wish to accept, you then send to UCAS to confirm the place. Bear in mind that Clearing places at top universities are scarce, and so you will need to act very quickly.

To: richard.martin@allington.ac.uk
From: Jonathan Luke
Subject: A level results

Dear Dr Martin
UCAS no 08-123456-7
I have just received my A level results, which were:
Mathematics A, Physics A, Economics C.
I also have a B grade in AS Philosophy.

I hold a conditional offer from Allington of ABB and I realise that my grades may not meet that offer. Nevertheless I am still determined to study engineering and I hope you will be able to find a place for me this year.

My head teacher supports my application and is emailing you a reference. Should you wish to contact him, his details are: Mr C. Harrow, tel: 0123 456 7891, fax: 0123 456 7892, email: c.harrow@edinburghhs.sch.uk.

Yours sincerely
Jonathan Luke

Adjustment

Students who have achieved grades that are better than the preditions on which both their firm and insurance choices were based have the opportunity to enter Adjustment. If this happens to you and you decide you would like to apply to an institution which asked for higher grades, you can put your application on hold for a short time (a week) in order to see if any of these institutions would be willing to offer you a place. When you register for Adjustment you do not lose your original offer so you are still able to accept this if you cannot find a course at another university.

Bear in mind that there are unlikely to be places on the most competitive courses available for Adjustment candidates, but it is still worth having a look if you are in this situation.

Retaking your A levels

If you decide to retake your A levels, it is likely that the examination requirements of your course will be higher than first time round. Most AS and some A2 units can be taken in January sittings, and some boards offer other sittings. This means that a January retake is often technically possible, although you should check carefully before taking up this option, since there may be complications because of, for example, coursework.

The timescale for your retake will depend on:

- the grades you obtained first time
- the availability of syllabuses in the January round of examinations.

If you simply need to improve one subject by one or two grades and can retake the exam on the same syllabus in January, then the short retake course is the logical option.

If, on the other hand, your grades were DDE and you took your exams through a board which has no mid-year retakes for the units that you require, you probably need to spend another year on your retakes. One-year courses are realistically the only option for students who do not achieve the required scores in International Baccalaureate or grades in the Cambridge Pre-University examinations.

Speak to your teachers about the implications of retaking your exams. Some independent sixth-form colleges provide specialist advice and teaching for students. Interviews to discuss this are free and carry no obligation to enrol on a course, so it is worth taking the time to talk to their staff before you embark on A level retakes. Many further education colleges also offer (usually one-year) retake courses, and some schools will allow students to return to resit subjects, either as external examination candidates or by repeating a year.

7| Further training, qualifications and careers

There is no 'typical' day for a working engineer. One of the attractions of engineering as a career is that you are, with suitable planning, able to follow a career path that suits your own individual skills and ambitions. If you like working outdoors, working as an on-site civil engineer would allow you to do this, whereas if you enjoy working in a laboratory then you might choose to be a structural, or electronic engineer. As we saw in the introduction to this book, engineers can work as part of a large team for a multinational engineering company or on their own in their own company. Engineers who are interested in planning and finance can work as product engineers, assessing the economic viability of manufacturing a product and then designing the production line.

Some students with engineering degrees decide to change direction after graduating. For example, engineers are highly sought after in the financial sector because an engineering degree demonstrates that the student has analytical and problem-solving skills.

The engineering institutes (see list in Chapter 9) and university engineering departments provide a good starting point for further investigation through the case histories that they publish. As an example, the Royal Academy of Engineering's case history booklet (www.raeng.org. uk/education/stf/pdf/tsz_fok_booklet.pdf) features a wide range of examples of the career paths followed by engineering graduates. Here are two of them.

Emily Cummins

At the age of 19, Emily Cummins was named Technology Woman of the Future for her award-winning invention – a sustainable solar-powered fridge that she designed for her A2 level project. She was the youngest nominee for this prestigious award and was also a short-listed finalist for the Audi Designer of the Year 2005. During her gap year Emily went to Africa and tested her fridge as a way of storing medicines in parts of the country where electricity is in short supply. She has just secured funding of £12,000 from NESTA's Ignite! Creative Spark Programme to further develop her product.

> 'At the age of four my granddad gave me . . . a hammer! And from then on whenever I visited him I spent hours with him in his hut watching and helping him take scrap materials and turn them into magnificent toys for me and my cousins. I love being creative, which was why I chose product design as one of my A level subjects. For my other subjects each lesson was the same . . . sit down, get out the text book, listen to the teacher for half an hour, then read the appendix and answer the questions below. I found them difficult and boring and most often found myself looking out of the window watching the world go by! Product design was different – I enjoyed the freedom of being able to research, develop and produce a product of my choice and could excel because I got to be creative. I like thinking out of the box – it gives me a huge buzz!

> 'I was put forward by my teacher for the Sustainable Design Award competition for a sustainable water carrier I designed for my AS project and was asked to attend a national conference held in Sheffield. I learnt a lot about the effect of burning fossil fuels and global warming and the importance of sustainability in the future. So I decided to make a sustainable refrigerator, which didn't use electricity, for my A2 level project. The idea was very simple – it consisted of a double cylinder and I put dampened sheep wool in between the cylinders. As the outside heat evaporated the water from the sheep wool the content was cooled. I tested my fridge prototype in Africa in my gap year and was able to achieve cooling to 7°C without any electricity. I would like to see my fridge being used to store medicine in places where electricity is not available.

> 'I believe the future of our world lies in designs produced within the next 50 years. Unless alternative sources of energy are produced or products are designed/redesigned using different techniques to power them other than electricity, the effects of global warming or the supplies of fossil fuels will mean that within 50 years any products that do not consider energy usage will be no good to us. Furthermore, I want engineers to use the new ways of providing energy to promote health.'

Reproduced with the kind permission of The Royal Academy of Engineering; www.raeng.org.uk/education/stf/pdf/tsz_fok_booklet.pdf

Kevin Warwick

Kevin Warwick is Professor of Cybernetics at the University of Reading. He was born in Coventry and left school to join British Telecom at the age of 16. At 22 he took his first degree at Aston University, followed by a PhD and a research post at Imperial College London. He is currently researching on direct interfaces between computer systems and the human nervous system. He undertook a set of experiments known as 'Project Cyborg', in which he had a chip implanted into his arm with the aim of upgrading the human body.

'The film I, Robot may seem like science fiction, but it is certainly foreseeable that machine intelligence has the ability to outperform human intelligence in the near future. Humans have limited capabilities. We sense the world in a restricted way, with vision being the best of the senses. We can only think in three dimensions, but it is believed that the universe has as many as eleven dimensions. Our communication method is slow and error prone; whereas machines can transfer information at speeds thousands of times quicker than our capability.

'As an artificial intelligence and control engineer, I carried out a research project named Cyborg, short for Cybernetic Organism, part human part machine. The project was in two phases. In the first phase I had a neurosurgical chip implanted into my left arm and it allowed a computer to monitor my movement in the department building. I could open doors, switch on lights and heaters or operate computers without any physical contact. In the second phase we went one step further; we implanted a similar chip into my wife and we attempted to create a new form of communication between our nervous systems via the internet. We explored how the internet could enhance our discovery in the first phase. An artificial hand was sent to New York and via the internet I was able to control the movement of the hand by thought alone!

'For the next 50 years, I want engineers to challenge the limit of the human body using technology. We have already demonstrated the possibility of connecting between nervous systems to computer systems. But can we do better? Can we power the brain-computer interface using energy from the human alone? Can we transmit emotions? Is telepathy possible? Engineers of the future will be able to provide us with the answers.'

Reproduced with the kind permission of The Royal Academy of Engineering; www.raeng.org.uk/education/stf/pdf/tsz_fok_booklet.pdf

In its booklet *Educating Engineers for the 21st Century*, the Royal Academy of Engineering provides an overview of what qualities future engineers will need to possess:

> 'No factor is more critical in underpinning the continuing health and vitality of any national economy than a strong supply of graduate engineers equipped with the understanding, attitudes and abilities necessary to apply their skills in business and other environments.
>
> Today, business environments increasingly require engineers who can design and deliver to customers not merely isolated products but complete solutions involving complex integrated systems. Increasingly they also demand the ability to work in globally dispersed teams across different time zones and cultures. The traditional disciplinary boundaries inherited from the 19th century are now being transgressed by new industries and disciplines, such as medical engineering and nanotechnology, which also involve the application of more recent engineering developments, most obviously the information and communication technologies. Meanwhile new products and services that would be impossible without the knowledge and skills of engineers – for instance the internet and mobile telephones – have become pervasive in our everyday life, especially for young people.
>
> Engineering businesses now seek engineers with abilities and attributes in two broad areas – technical understanding and enabling skills. The first of these comprises: a sound knowledge of disciplinary fundamentals; a strong grasp of mathematics; creativity and innovation; together with the ability to apply theory in practice. The second is the set of abilities that enable engineers to work effectively in a business environment: communication skills; teamworking skills; and business awareness of the implications of engineering decisions and investments. It is this combination of understanding and skills that underpins the role that engineers now play in the business world, a role with three distinct, if interrelated, elements: that of the technical specialist imbued with expert knowledge; that of the integrator able to operate across boundaries in complex environments; and that of the change agent providing the creativity, innovation and leadership necessary to meet new challenges.
>
> Engineering today is characterised by both a rapidly increasing diversity of the demands made on engineers in their professional lives and the ubiquity of the products and services they provide. Yet there is a growing concern that in the UK the education system responsible for producing new generations of engineers is failing to keep pace with the inherent dynamism of this situation and indeed with the increasing need for engineers.'

Chartered engineer status

Chartered Engineer (CEng) is a professional title registered by the Engineering Council. Engineers who achieve this status have been able to demonstrate that they have reached a high level of professional competence. Attaining the status of Chartered Engineer brings many benefits, including:

- being part of an elite group of highly qualified engineers
- professional recognition of your qualifications and attainments
- higher earnings potential
- improved career prospects
- international recognition of your academic and professional qualifications
- access to continual professional training.

The normal route towards gaining the qualification is (see Figure 3):

1. an accredited bachelor's degree (BEng)
2. a master's degree (MEng)
3. membership of one of the professional engineering institutes
4. experience of professional practice.

It usually takes between eight and 12 years from the start of an undergraduate degree to reach CEng status. For more details, contact the Engineering Council or one of the engineering institutes (see list on pp. 95–97).

Master's courses

Many undergraduate engineering courses are four years in length, and lead to a master's qualification (MEng), rather than a bachelor's degree (BEng). The alternative route to a postgraduate qualification is by taking a self-contained MEng course after completing the bachelor's degree. Master's degrees allow students to focus their studies on a specific area of engineering. Applications for self-contained postgraduate courses are usually done directly to the universities, rather than through a central scheme. For listings of master's courses, see www.prospects.ac.uk and the university websites.

The advantages of doing a master's course are:

- greater specialisation
- better job prospects
- higher earning potential.

The cost of a master's course varies from university to university, but is likely to be in the range £14,000–£18,000 per year for tuition fees. A number of grants and scholarships are available (see p. 25).

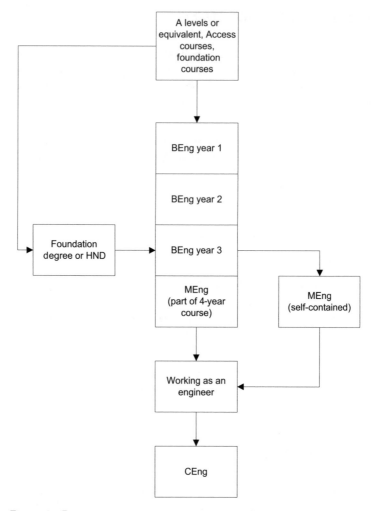

Figure 3: Routes to gaining an engineering qualification

The structure of a master's course will depend on where and what you study. As an example, here is the course programme for the MSc Aerospace Engineering course at the University of Bath.

- Aerodynamics
- Aircraft performance and design
- Control systems
- Heat transfer
- Thermofluid systems
- Aircraft propulsion
- Aircraft stability and control
- Experimental techniques in aerodynamics

- Aerospace structures
- Computational fluid dynamics
- Finite element analysis
- Composite materials
- Engineering and project management
- Research and design methods
- Practical instrumentation techniques
- Dissertation

Source: www.bath.ac.uk

8 | Current issues

As a potential university engineering student you need to demonstrate your interest by keeping up to date with current issues and developments. Engineering is an ever-evolving subject, with new materials, processes and products being developed every day. Just think about the rapid changes in the field of communication over the past 15 years, for example. Once you have identified your particular areas of interest, you need to keep up to date with your research and reading, perhaps keeping a scrapbook, physical or on your computer, of news articles that are relevant to your chosen area of study, and using this as part of your preparation for an interview.

In this chapter, I have summarised some news stories and developments that were current towards the end of 2010. By the time you read these, there will have been many more. The summaries in this chapter are therefore included to give you an illustration of the kind of events and other news items you should be reading about. In other words, they are a starting point for your own research, rather than being an easily accessible source of information to memorise prior to your interviews.

Engineering disasters

By the time you read this, there will almost certainly have been more recent examples of situations where avoidable (due to human error or faulty materials) or unavoidable (due to, for example, weather conditions or natural phenomena) disasters either affect engineering projects or require engineers to rectify the situation or save lives. In 2010 there were two notable examples of this.

Chilean miners

The partial collapse of the San José copper and gold mine in Chile in August 2010 trapped 33 miners 700m underground. Engineers first drilled some narrow boreholes to allow microphones to be lowered in the hope of detecting whether the miners were alive and, if so, where they were. After 17 days, they received a note from the miners attached to one of the probes. The next stage was to supply the miners with food, water, medicines, clothing and beds – all through the boreholes.

As the tunnels leading to where the miners were sheltering were blocked, engineers decided to drill three holes into the mine, wide enough to be able to winch the miners up. Three different types of drilling were planned – two involved drilling pilot holes which could then be widened and strengthened, and the third was planned to use oil drilling equipment to make a hole wide enough for the winching capsule without the need for a pilot hole. All three holes were drilled at the same time, to ensure that the rescue attempt would not be disrupted if there was a problem with a particular hole or piece of equipment. The first drill to reach the miners was the second of the pilot drills (named 'Plan B') which broke through in early October. The hole was then widened and strengthened with steel tubes, and a specially designed capsule was then lowered down to the miners. The miners were finally brought to the surface in November.

The rescue primarily involved: mining engineers, mechanical engineers.

BP oil spill

In April 2010, an explosion on the Deepwater Horizon drilling rig operated by BP in the Gulf of Mexico killed 11 people, and the resulting oil leak caused environmental damage to many hundreds of kilometres of the coastline. The well was eventually sealed in July of the same year. It is estimated that around five million barrels of oil were released into the environment. It has been suggested that the sealant used to seal the well after the drilling had begun (a 'foam slurry' made up of cement and nitrogen gas) had previously failed a number of safety tests.

Various solutions were proposed, including using explosives to seal the vent, but were ruled out. A number of attempts to cap the leak were made. In May, it was decided to drill relief wells close to the original borehole so that when the well could be capped, cement and mud could be pumped into the borehole to permanently seal it. Because of the pressure of the oil under the sea bed, it was decided to try to place a cap over the well which was connected to pipes that could carry the oil and gas directly to ships. The first attempts were partially successful. A later attempt, in July used a more secure cap (called 'Top Hat Number 10'). Tests using cement and mud began in August 2010, and the well was eventually sealed in September.

The attempts to stop the oil spill and restrict the damage to the environment primarily involved: oil and gas engineers, mechanical engineers, marine engineers.

The world's tallest building

The Burj Khalifa, in Dubai, was completed in September 2009. It has a height of 512m and foundations around 50m deep. It is estimated that nearly 400,000m^3 of concrete and 39 million kg of steel were used in its construction. For a building this tall, many factors had to be taken into account when designing it. Not only did the materials have to be strong enough to support the weight of the building, but also the design had to incorporate flexibility in order to cope with high winds. The building used a buttress system to provide extra strength and stability, just as medieval cathedrals had done 500 years earlier. The main structural elements of the building are steel and concrete, with a glass and aluminium façade. Concrete can be made to many different specifications, and engineers had to plan what types to use for the foundations (which need to be dense and impervious to moisture) and for the main core of the building (which must be able to withstand tensile and torsional stresses in addition to compressive forces and needs to be less dense than the foundations). Systems had to be designed to pump concrete up to 600m above the ground, and to ensure that the setting time was neither too short nor too long.

The construction of the tower primarily involved: structural engineers, materials engineers, civil engineers, mechanical engineers, electrical engineers.

Rare earth elements

Not many people had heard of rare earth elements prior to late 2010. Elements such as dysprosium, terbium, neodymium, lanthanum and gadolinium do not usually make front page news. But these and 12 other elements, the so-called 'rare earths', are essential in the construction of computer memory, lighting, electric motors, hybrid batteries for cars, fibre-optics and many more of the things that define our lives. Why did these elements make headlines in 2010? Because over 95% of the world's supplies are mined in China, and China has hinted that because of its own requirements, it may stop exporting them in 2012. These elements can be found in other parts of the world but building mines to extract them takes time and this will leave a gap of a few years when rare earths are likely to be less available to the world.

Engineers involved in the excavation and application of rare earth elements: mining engineers, electrical engineers, chemical engineers, electronic engineers, production engineers, mechanical engineers.

Alternative sources of energy

Engineers use energy to create their products, and to run them. Engineers also create the structures and processes that produce usable energy. Engineers, therefore, are at the forefront of the search to develop new energy sources. As well as being finite sources of energy (in other words, they will one day run out, or at the very least, become uneconomical to extract), fossil fuels cause environmental damage and are closely linked to climate change and global warming. Many fields of engineering have an interest in developing *alternative* or *renewable* energy sources. While there are no set definitions of these words, they generally refer to energy sources that do not involve fossil fuels and/or those whose consumption does not deplete the planet's natural the resources or reserves.

Alternative energy sources that are currently used commercially are:

- geothermal energy
- hydroelectric power
- nuclear fission
- solar power (solar panels to produce heat, photovoltaic cells that create electricity from sunlight)
- tidal power, biomass (using bacteria to produce gas through digestion of organic materials, making fuels out of natural materials such as palm oil)
- wave power
- wind power.

An alternative energy source that is in development is nuclear fusion.

There are a number of ways of categorising energy sources (see Tables 2 and 3).

Table 2 Categorisation of energy sources based on origin

Energy source derived from sun	Energy source not derived from sun
Solar	Geothermal
Wind (heat from the sun creates areas of low and high pressure, causing wind)	Nuclear fusion
Wave (winds cause waves in the sea)	Nuclear fission
Fossil fuels (coal, oil, gas, etc. were once living things)	Tidal
Hydroelectric (water sources, such as rivers, were created by precipitation of rain, caused by the sun's heating)	
Biomass	

Engineers primarily involved in developing alternative energy sources: electrical engineers, electronic engineers, bio-engineers, mechanical engineers, geo-engineers, chemical engineers.

Table 3 Categorisation of energy sources based on affect on source

Renewable*	Non-renewable
Solar	Fossil fuels
Wind	Nuclear fission
Wave	Geothermal
Tidal	
Hydroelectric	
Biomass (since although the individual sources cannot be used again once the energy is extracted, the supply can be maintained by, for example, planting more oil palms)	
Nuclear fusion (considered renewable since the likely source would be sea water which is effectively inexhaustible)	

* By 'renewable' we generally mean that the source of the energy is unaffected by the extraction of energy. For example, every time coal is burned there is less coal remaining on the Earth, whereas if a wind turbine creates electricity it does not affect the source (movement of air, which is caused by solar heating).

Engineering business case histories

Try to keep up to date with stories associated with engineering businesses and entrepreneurs. Most new engineering projects and developments are driven by commercial companies that want to sell their products or processes; and while some new devices are developed by university research departments, these are often funded by industry.

The list below aims to provide you with a starting point for your research, as there will undoubtedly be new names that will become more relevant by the time you read this book.

- Apple's iPad, iPod and iPhone
- The Android operating system for mobile devices
- Google
- Inventors and entrepreneurs such as Sir James Dyson
- Virgin Galactic
- Multinational construction companies such as Arup
- Aeronautical engineering companies such as BAE Systems
- Biotech companies such as Amgen
- Oil and petroleum companies that are developing alternative or renewable sources of energy, such as Chevron
- Engineering companies involved in the 2012 London Olympic Games, such as Atkins.

9 | Further information

The UCAS tariff

Tables 4–7 reproduced by kind permission of UCAS.

Table 4 Combinations of grades and total 360 points

A level	AS level
AAB	E
ABB	C
BBB	A

Table 5 International Baccalaureate tariff points

IB Grade	Tariff points
45	720
44	698
43	676
42	654
41	632
40	611
39	589
38	567
37	545
36	523
35	501
34	479
33	457
32	435
31	413
30	392
29	370
28	348
27	350
26	326
25	303
24	280

Table 6 Irish Leaving Certificate tariff points

Grade		Tariff points
Higher	Ordinary	
A1		90
A2		77
B1		71
B2		64
B3		58
C1		52
C2		45
C3	A1	39
D1		33
D2	A2	26
D3	B1	20
	B2	14
	B3	7

Table 7 Scottish Highers tariff points

Advanced Higher		Higher		Scottish Interdisciplinary Project		Scottish National Certificate	
Grade	Tariff points	Grade	Tariff points	Grade	Tariff points	Grade	Tariff points
A	130	A	80	A	65	A	125
B	110	B	65	B	55	B	100
C	90	C	50	C	45	C	75
D	72	D	36				

Useful contacts

University applications and funding

www.ucas.com
www.direct.gov.uk
www.slc.co.uk

News

www.bbc.co.uk
www.guardian.co.uk

Organisations for Engineers in the UK

Engineering Council
www.engc.org.uk

British Computer Society (BCS)
www.bcs.org

Chartered Institution of Building Services Engineers (CIBSE)
www.cibse.org

Chartered Institution of Highways & Transportation (CIHT)
www.ciht.org.uk

Chartered Institute of Plumbing and Heating Engineering (CIPHE)
www.ciphe.org.uk

Chartered Institution of Water and Environmental Management (CIWEM)
www.ciwem.org.uk

Energy Institute (EI)
www.energyinst.org.uk

Institute of Acoustics (IOA)
www.ioa.org.uk

Institute of Cast Metals Engineers (ICME)
www.icme.org.uk

Institute of Highway Engineers (IHE)
www.theihe.org

Institute of Marine Engineering, Science and Technology (IMarEST)
www.imarest.org

Institute of Measurement and Control (InstMC)
www.instmc.org.uk

Institute of Materials, Minerals and Mining (IoM³)
www.iom3.org

Institute of Physics (IOP)
www.iop.org

Institute of Physics and Engineering in Medicine (IPEM)
www.ipem.ac.uk

Institute of Water (IWO)
www.instituteofwater.org.uk

Institution of Agricultural Engineers (IAgrE)
www.iagre.org

Institution of Civil Engineers (ICE)
www.ice.org.uk

Institution of Chemical Engineers (IChemE)
www.icheme.org

Institution of Diesel and Gas Turbine Engineers (IDGTE)
www.idgte.org

Institution of Engineering Designers (IED)
www.ied.org.uk

Institution of Engineering and Technology (IET)
www.theiet.org

Institution of Fire Engineers (IFE)
www.ife.org.uk

Institution of Gas Engineers and Managers (IGEM)
www.igem.org.uk

Institution of Lighting Engineers (ILE)
www.ile.co.uk

Institution of Mechanical Engineers (IMechE)
www.imeche.org

Institution of Royal Engineers (InstRE)
www.instre.org

Institution of Structural Engineers (IStructE)
www.istructe.org

Nuclear Institute (NI)
www.nuclearinst.com

Royal Academy of Engineering
www.raeng.org.uk

Royal Aeronautical Society (RAeS)
www.aerosociety.com

Royal Institution of Naval Architects (RINA)
www.rina.org.uk

Society of Environmental Engineers (SEE)
www.environmental.org.uk

Society of Operations Engineers (SOE)
www.soe.org.uk

The Welding Institute (TWI)
www.twi.co.uk

Specialist engineering publications

Aviation Week
www.aviationweek.com

Nano
www.nanomagazine.co.uk

Race Car Engineering
www.racecar-engineering.com

Engineering News Record
www.enr.com

New Civil Engineer
www.nce.co.uk

The Engineer
www.theengineer.co.uk

Books

Engineering

- Blockley, David, *Bridges: The science and art of the world's most inspiring structures*. Oxford: OUP, 2010.
- Brenner, Brian, ed., *Don't Throw This Away!: The civil engineering life*. Reston, VA: American Society of Civil Engineers, 2006.
- Dupre, Judith, *Skyscrapers: A history of the world's most extraordinary buildings*. New York, NY: Black Dog & Leventhal Publishers Inc, 2008.
- Dyson, James, *Against the Odds: An autobiography*. London: Orion, 1997.
- Eberhart, Mark E., *Why Things Break: Understanding the world by the way it comes apart*. New York, NY:Three Rivers Press, 2005.
- Gordon, J.E., *Structures: Or why things don't fall down*. London: Penguin, 1991.

- Gordon, J.E., *The New Science of Strong Materials: Or why you don't fall through the floor.* London: Penguin Science, 1991.
- Linzmayer, Owen, *Apple Confidential 2.0: The definitive history of the world's most colorful company, the real story of Apple Computer, Inc.* San-Francisco, CA: No Starch Press, 2004.
- Michell, Tony, *Samsung Electronics and the Struggle for Leadership of the Electronics Industry.* Chichester: John Wiley & Sons, 2010.
- Petroski, Henry, *Invention by Design: How engineers get from thought to thing.* Cambridge, MA: Harvard University Press, 1998.

Thinking skills

Butterworth, John and Thwaites, Geoff, *Thinking Skills.* Cambridge: CUP, 2005.